HUMMINGBIRDS

HUMMINGBIRDS

Sara Godwin

MALLARD PRESS

MALLARD PRESS
An imprint of BDD Promotional Book Company, Inc.
666 Fifth Avenue
New York, New York 10103

A FRIEDMAN GROUP BOOK

Published by MALLARD PRESS
An imprint of BDD Promotional Book Company, Inc.
666 Fifth Avenue
New York, New York 10103

Mallard Press and its accompanying design and logo are trademarks
of BDD Promotional Book Company, Inc.

Copyright © 1991 by Michael Friedman Publishing Group, Inc.

First published in the United States of America in 1991 by
Mallard Press.

ISBN 0-7924-5510-X

HUMMINGBIRDS
was prepared and produced by
Michael Friedman Publishing Group, Inc.
15 West 26th Street
New York, New York 10010

Editor: Elizabeth Viscott Sullivan
Designer: Marcena Mulford
Layout: Benjamin Chase
Art Director: Jeff Batzli
Photography Editor: Christopher C. Bain

Typeset by The Interface Group, Inc.
Color separation by Scantrans Pte Ltd.
Printed and bound in Hong Kong by Leefung-Asco Printers, Ltd.

Dedication

To C.J., who gives me strange and wonderful gifts, like dozens of hummingbirds, delivered to the door. (Well, to the window, to be perfectly precise.)

Acknowledgements

No one writes a book alone. There are always other contributors whose names do not appear on the title page. Among these, I wish to thank my grandmother, Jane Murray Godwin, who wakened my interest in bird-watching by sitting me at her window to watch red cardinals in the snow; the intelligent, knowledgeable women who helped me become a docent at the Audubon Canyon Ranch in Bolinas, California, by generously sharing their impressive range of information about birds; to Dr. Steve Bailey of the Natural History Museum at the California Academy of Sciences, who sat on the floor with me patiently examining drawer after drawer of hummingbird nests and, equally patiently, answering innumerable questions; to Dr. F. Ray Fosberg, Botanist Emeritus and taxonomist *par excellence*, of the Smithsonian Institution, who helped immeasurably in sorting English, Spanish, and Amerindian flower names into their proper Latin equivalents; to all of the people who over the years have helped me travel the world, birding all the way, most especially Overseas Adventure Travel of Cambridge, Massachusetts, who got me to the Andes in Ecuador; to those living wonders, the hummingbirds themselves; and to my husband, whose enthusiasm for the book was so great that he hung hummingbird feeders at every window so that every time I looked up from researching or writing to stare out the window, I was observing hummingbird behavior. Thanks to him, I now have an embarrassing number of hours of hummingbird observation to my credit. To these, then, goes my warmest appreciation; all errors, God forbid, are exclusively my own.

Contents

Chapter One

HISTORY, MYTH, AND LEGEND: "AS GLORIOUS AS THE RAINEBOWE…"

"*As Glorious as the Rainebowe...*"

Hummingbirds' names are perhaps among the loveliest combination of words on earth. Even if one has never been blessed by the sight of one of these winged wonders, their names alone are enough to spark the imagination. How could anyone resist the Spangled Coquette *(Lophornis strictolopha)*, the Blue-chinned Sapphire *(Chlorestes notatus)*, the Glittering-throated Emerald *(Amazilia fimbriata)*, the Crowned Woodnymph *(Thalurnia furcata)*, the Glistening Sunangel *(Heliangelus luminosus)*, the Empress Brilliant *(Heliodoxa imperatrix)*, the Fiery Topaz *(Topaza pyra)*, the Rainbow-bearded Thornbill *(Chalcostigma herrani)*, the Little Woodstar *(Acestrura bombus)*, or the Shining Sunbeam *(Aglaeactis cupripennis)?*

Of the 8,700 species of birds on earth, roughly half of them are songbirds (passerines). The other half, into which the hummingbirds fall, are non-passerines. Of the 4,350 non-passerines, hummingbirds are the largest family, with 338 known species. While 2 of these species live in North America (Allen's *[Selasphorus sasin]* and Anna's *[Calypte anna]*), and 14 migrate there, all 338 species are found in Central and South America. Hummingbirds are exclusively a New World (Neotropical) species; they are found only in the Americas.

The Magnificent (Rivoli) Hummingbird is one of the largest hummingbirds, though it is only 4½ to 5 inches (11.25 to 12.5 cm) long. It is twice as big as the Bee Hummingbird of Cuba, which is the smallest bird in the world at a tiny 2½ inches (6.25 cm). Most hummingbirds are less than 4 inches (10 cm) from tip to tail, shorter than a bald eagle's middle toe.

No one knows where hummingbirds came from, in the paleontological or evolutionary sense, for no fossils have ever been found. No one knows how many species of hummingbirds there are, despite the fact that they have been placed in their own order, Trochilidae, and number more species than any other single family in the Northern Hemisphere, except the American flycatcher, which has 367 species.

While hummingbirds are already the largest non-passerine family of birds, the current tally of the family Trochilidae, with its 338 species and 116 genera, is considered by no means complete. Much of the area in which they are most likely to be found — ranging from cloud forests to valleys 15,000 feet (4,500 m) into the Andes to equatorial rain forest — has never been properly explored and mapped, much less thoroughly searched for new hummingbird species.

The greatest number of hummingbirds are found within five degrees latitude on either side of the equatorial belt, a strip of ten degrees latitude that stretches across the widest part of South America. At the furthest reaches of the hummingbird's range, both north and south, there is only one species. At the northern extreme, the Rufous Hummingbird *(Selasphorus rufus)* migrates to Alaska; at the southern extreme, the Green-backed Firecrown *(Sephanoides sephanoides)* migrates almost to the edge of Antarctica at Tierra del Fuego.

In terms of distribution, there are 163 species found in Ecuador, 135 in Colombia, 100 in Peru, 97 in Venezuela, 90 in Brazil, 54 in Costa Rica, 51 in Mexico, 19 in the Caribbean, 16 in the United States (only one of which, the Ruby-throated Hummingbird *[Archilochus colubris]*, is found east of the Rocky Mountains), and 4 in Canada. South of the equator, Chile has 7 species, Uruguay 4, and Tierra del Fuego, 1, the previously mentioned Green-backed Firecrown.

Because they are tiny, it is tempting to think of hummingbirds as delicate. In fact, they are tiny, tough, and well adapted to both very high elevations and very low temperatures. The majority of hummingbird species live in the high Andes, where temperatures swiftly fall to freezing and below at night. Some even live on the edge of the perpetual snows of Cotopaxi, Chimborazo, Sangay, and other towering, snow-capped peaks of the Andes. Many of those that migrate into the United States and Canada follow the lines of the mountain ranges which extend across both continents, from the Andes to the Sierra Nevada of Mexico, to the Rocky Mountains of the United States and Canada, or the Sierra Nevada of California.

Hummingbirds were one of the great wonders of the New World, and were described with equal breathlessness by Columbus and Cortés. In his log entry for October 21, 1492, Columbus wrote: "Little birds...so different from ours it is a marvel." Next to the drab sparrows of Spain, these darting, dashing atoms of aerial iridescence were indeed a marvel.

Arthur Cleveland Bent, who wrote the Life Histories of North American Birds, *some twenty volumes worth, for the Smithsonian Institution in the 1930s, described the tiny sprite that is the Rufous Hummingbird in glowing terms: "The brilliant scarlet of the rufous hummer's gorget, which often glows like burnished gold, puts it in the front rank as a gleaming gem, a feathered ball of fire."*

The Purple-throated Carib is found in the Lesser Antilles, the small islands of the Caribbean off the coast of Venezuela, including Trinidad, Tobago, and Barbados.

The Streamertail, whose Latin name is Trochilus polytmus, *is a curious anomaly of scientific classification. Originally used by Herodotus to describe a small plover, the word* Trochilos *means runner. Aristotle borrowed the word to describe the smallest bird he knew, the kinglet. Linnaeus latinized the word to* Trochilus *to use for hummingbird classification, though no bird on earth is less likely to run. But Aristotle had used the word for a bird he described as very small, and hummingbirds are certainly very small. Eight of the sixteen hummingbirds found in North America, and a number of others as well, were once classified as* Trochilus, *but today only the Streamertail carries the name.*

An Italian scholar in Queen Isabella's court, Pietro Martire de Anghiera, read Columbus's reports avidly and wrote to his friends in Italy of birds in the New World that were even smaller than warblers and winter wrens. In 1514 Pope Leo X received a preserved hummingbird skin; the artist Raphael, probably working directly from the skin, painted a pair of hummingbirds on the eleventh pillar of an arcade in the Vatican that was completed in 1519. Raphael's portrait is the first known depiction of the hummingbird in Europe.

Not until fifteen years later, in 1534, did the first written description of the hummingbird appear. In his *De la Natural Historia de las Indias*, Gonzalo Fernandez de Oviedo y Valdes wrote:

> *No bigger than a man's thumb...and of such swiftness in flight, that you cannot see the movement of their wings. The colors shine like those of the little birds artists paint to illuminate the margins of holy books...and with a bill as delicate as a fine needle. They are hardy, yet so little, I would not dare tell of it if others had not seen them also...*

By 1555 Oviedo's report had been published in Spanish, Latin, French, and English, and was read eagerly throughout Europe.

Those who went to the New World to report on its fabulous richness heard stories of the hummingbirds' ability to return from the dead from the Aztecs, and dutifully sent the stories home. In 1550 Bernardino de Sahagun wrote that hummingbirds die each winter and somehow resurrect themselves with the returning warmth of spring: "It awakens, comes to life." The historian Antonio Herrera summarized the New World reports on the hummingbird in 1601:

> *There are some birds in this country the size of butterflies, with long beaks and brilliant plumage...Like the bees, they live on flowers and the dew which settles on them. And when the rainy season is over and the dry weather sets in, they fasten themselves to a tree by their beaks, and soon die. But in the following season when the rains return, they come to life again.*

In 1651 the *Penny Cyclopedia* amplified Herrera's story by writing that hummingbirds:

> *were supposed to live longer than the flowers which afforded them food; and, when those flowers faded, they were believed to fix themselves by the bill to some pine or other tree, and there remain during the dreary months till the descending rains brought back the spring, when they revived again to undergo the same alternation of life and death.*

The hummingbirds' apparent ability to die and return to life is now known as torpor. Torpor occurs when the weather is cold by hummingbird standards; its function is to help the birds conserve energy. Hummingbirds become torpid by lowering their body temperature to within a few degrees of air temperature and slowing their metabolism to one-fiftieth of the rate normal for a bird perching quietly. Ordinarily, torpor lasts only overnight (and is often referred to as noctivation); the rise in temperature in the morning allows the birds to resume their normal activities.

Since the temperatures in the Andes and Ecuador, where the vast majority of hummingbirds are found, often approach freezing at high altitude, the native peoples were familiar with the phenomenon of torpor; the women knew how to revive the tiny birds by warming them between their breasts. The Spanish missionaries of the seventeenth century used the hummingbird's torpor to explain the concept of the resurrection of Jesus to the natives of the New World. (For more on torpor, see p. 44.)

The conquistadors must have gaped in wonder when they first laid eyes on the mighty Aztec king, Montezuma, whose robes of state flashed with the brilliant iridescence of hummingbird plumage. While many of today's brides pick out the prettiest of alençon laces for their wedding gowns and bejewel them with seed pearls and sequins,

Pages 14–15: The Aztecs worshipped a hummingbird god, Huitzilpochtli, whose name combined the words for hummingbird and wizard. The god was believed to turn the souls of soldiers into hummingbirds, suggesting that the hummingbirds then seemed as eager to pick a fight with each other as they are today. Also shown is the god named for the quetzalcoatl, *the resplendant quetzal, still found from Mexico to Panama.*

Below: Hummingbirds use their tiny feet to perch, and that's about all. They rarely walk more than a step or two.

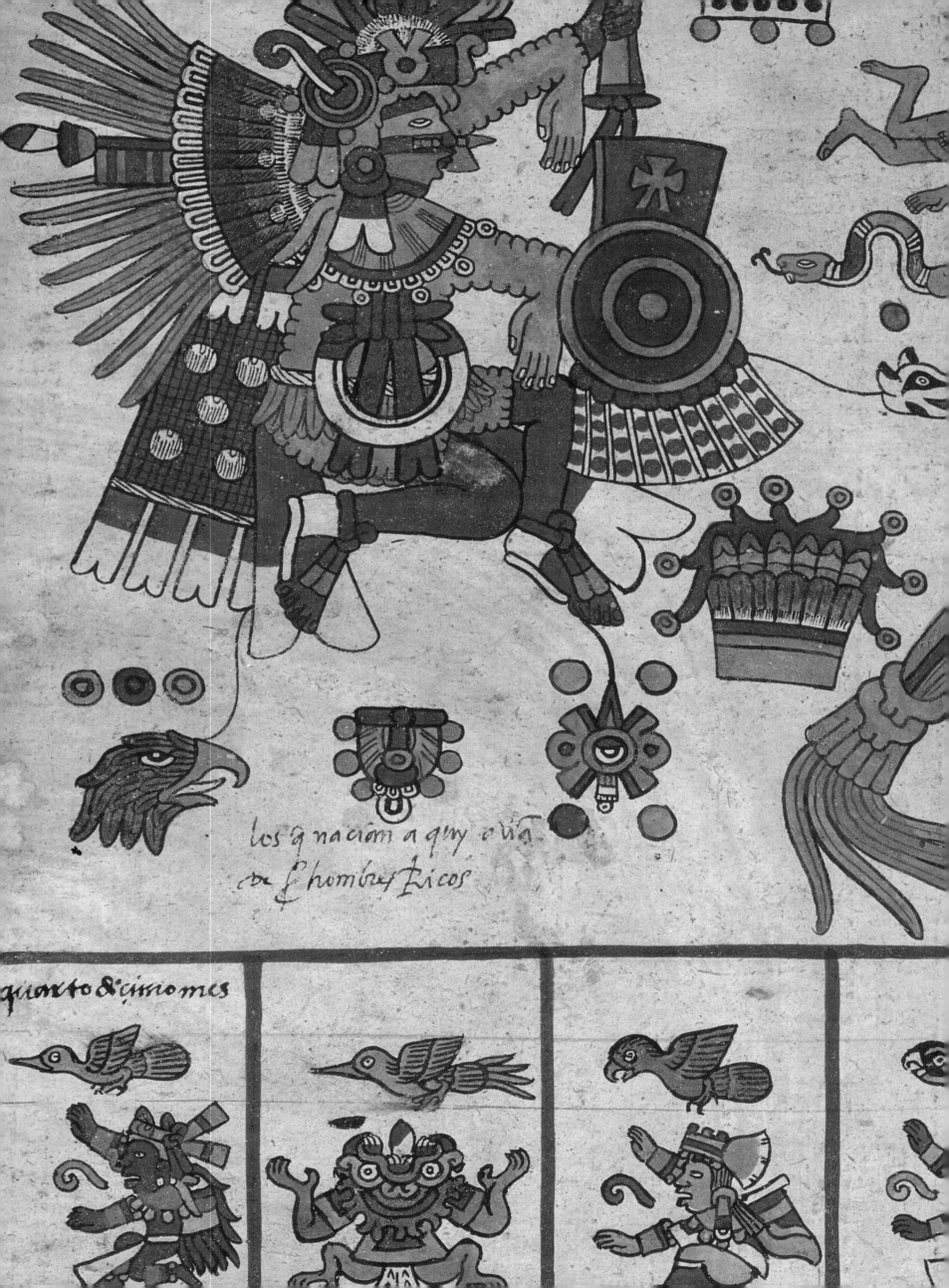

los q̃ nacion a q̃y ol̃lã
de f hombr̃ Ricos

quarto d'çīnōmes

Below: Unlike most birds' wings, which are analogous to the human shoulder, elbow, and wrist, hummingbirds' wings are analogous to the human hand. The flight feathers are attached to what would be fingers. In effect, hummingbirds fly with their hands rather than their arms. All hummingbirds' wings have ten primary feathers, six or seven secondaries, and ten retrices (occasionally there may be fewer).

Aztec brides bedecked themselves with ornaments made from the sparkling feathers of hummingbirds. The Aztecs also wore bracelets of hummingbird feathers for good luck in love, war, and other games of chance. Hernando Cortés, leader of the Spanish conquistadors, sent back reports to the king and queen of Spain of tapestries he had seen depicting day-to-day Aztec life that were embroidered with the glittering, gleaming feathers of hummingbirds.

The Aztec god of war's intimidating name, Huitzilpochtli, is borrowed partly from the hummingbird's name *(huitzitzil)*; the latter half of the name *(-pochtli)* means wizard. The Aztecs honored the god by decorating statues of him with hummingbird skins. The Aztecs believed that Huitzilpochtli transformed fallen warriors into hummingbirds. The Toltecs, contemporaries of the Aztecs, also had a hummingbird wizard god, Tozcatlpoca. When the Aztecs defeated the Toltecs in battle, they took the statue of Tozcatlpoca to stand beside that of Huitzilpochtli.

Observing that hummingbirds were most likely to duel with each other at dawn and dusk, the Aztecs thought the birds fought off the powers of darkness, and helped the sun to return each day with light and warmth. In return for their help, the Aztecs believed, the sun gave hummingbirds bright jewels that flashed whenever they faced the sun. According to Virginia Holmgren's *The Way of the Hummingbird*, during a ceremonial dance intended to support the hummingbirds in their battle against the coming winter's darkness, the Aztecs chanted the song of the hummingbird:

Bird, warrior, and wizard, I am the shining one.
I have no equal; no, not even one.
Never in vain is my nightly battle done,
For mine is the magic that brings back the sun.

The dancers circled round and round, hand in hand, until the end of the ritual, when the men picked up the women by the waist and lifted them towards the sky to symbolize the hummingbird in flight.

Even in other languages the hummingbird's names are as lovely as their namesake. The other Aztec words for the hummingbird, *pigada* and *ourbiri*, mean "tresses of the day star" and "rays of the sun." In Spanish, the hummingbird is *la chuparosa*, "the rose sucker," or *la joya voladore*, "the flying jewel." In Portuguese, the bird is called *beija flor*, or "flower kisser." The English name comes not from the hummingbird's song—most hummingbirds may more accurately be said to squeak than sing—but from the humming sound of their whirring wings; in Creole, *murmures* is another onomatopoeic attempt to duplicate the sound of their swift wings.

The first American colonist to send reports of the hummingbird home to England was Captain John Smith, the man so shy that he tried to get his friend, Miles Standish, to propose for him, only to have Standish retort, "Speak for yourself, John." He did, at last, speak to the Algonquin chief Powhatan, and was rewarded with the hand of the Indian Princess, Pocahontas. Somehow, in the midst of these fascinating developments, Smith also wrote several volumes that appeared in London between 1608 and 1624; in one of these he described a hummingbird as "scarce so big as a wren, less than a kinglet." He also wrote that some of the birds were red, and that some were blue, although the only species he was likely to have seen, the Ruby-throated Hummingbird, is crimson and emerald green; perhaps Smith's vision was not much better than his self-esteem. One researcher has gone so far as to suggest that Smith was color-blind as well as shy in the extreme.

Smith may have first seen hummingbirds worn as an earring by Pocahontas's father, Chief Powhatan. Only those of the highest rank were permitted to wear the hummingbirds' brilliant plumage. This was true of the other tribes of northeastern America, like the Algonquin, of the Taino tribes of the Caribbean, and of the Aztecs of Mexico. This fact was remarked upon by one William Wood, a Massachusetts colonist, who wrote in *New England's Prospects* (1634) that an Indian chief might be easily identified by the hummingbird skin he wore as an ear pendant. Wood described the Ruby-throated Hummingbird as:

> one of the wonders of the Countrey, being no bigger than a Hornet, yet
> hath all the dimensions of a Bird, as a bill and wings with quills, Spider-
> like Legges, small clawes. For color shee is glorious as the Rainebowe, as
> shee flies shee makes a little humming noise like a humble bee; wherefore
> shee is called Humbird.

Opposite page, top: This stylized depiction of a hummingbird feeding from a flower was found in Mexico City, Mexico, and that of the hummingbird below was found in Vera-cruz, Mexico. When Montezuma ruled the Aztecs, Mexico City was a magnificent city of beautiful canals and lagoons, trees and gardens, and impressive causeways. Huge aviaries were filled with thousands of bright birds, including hummingbirds, quetzals, eagles, and flamingoes. In June 1520 Cortés, who had described Mexico City to Charles V of Spain as "the most beautiful city in the world," laid siege to the city. On June 16, 1520 Cortés made a military move calculated to horrify and terrify the Mexican people: He set fire to the aviaries.

Once called the Guianan King or King Hummingbird, this bird has come into a magnificent common name: It is now called the Crimson Topaz. It is found in South America from the Guianas to Ecuador.

The effort to make those far away understand how very small these astonishing new creatures were led explorers and colonists to rack their brains for appropriate comparisons. Hummingbirds were described as being no bigger than a hornet, a humble bee, and a great beetle. They were said to be so small and swift of wing that it was difficult to know if they were birds, or bees, or butterflies. They were compared in weight to the Spanish *tomine,* the smallest unit of measure for silver, and in Minsheu's *Spanish Dictionary* (1599) as weighing "near the weight of an English sixpence." James Lumden of Glasgow made a series of comparisons to describe the hummingbird to those who had never laid eyes on one. While his description was good, the illustration that accompanied it looked more like a snipe than a hummingbird. In 1794 he wrote:

> *The hummingbird is the least of all birds; the head, together with the feathers, is of the bigness of a mean-sized sweet cherry; the neck is three-quarters of an inch long; the body an inch and a quarter. The body together with the feathers, is scarce equal in bigness to a Spanish olive. Its color is wonderfully resplendent: A green (such as is seen on the necks of peacocks) with a golden flame color, and yellow, are so strangely mixed, that being exposed to the sunbeams, it shines admirably. It makes its nest in the boughs of trees, of the bigness of a Holland schilling, and lays very white eggs: two, for the most part, of an oval figure, not bigger than peas. It is fed and nourished with honeydew, and the juice of flowers, which it sucks out of them with its bill. It flies very swift and makes a humming noise, like a hornet or bee; hence it took its name in English of Hummingbird.*

Allen's Humming Bird.
SCALED PARTRIDGE.
CATBIRD.
SCREECH OWL

Left: Allen's Hummingbird, whose Latin name is Selasphorus sasin, *breeds in the United States, only along the coast of California and just over the border into Oregon. Difficult to distinguish from the Rufous, the Latin name* sasin *is the Nootka Indian word for hummingbird, recorded by Captain James Cook in 1778 as applying to the Rufous. (The Allen's does not breed far enough north to have been found in Nootka Territory.) The English name, Allen's Hummingbird, comes from Charles Allen (1841–1930), the first American to describe the differences between the Allen's and the Rufous. The bird was originally classified in 1829 by the great French hummingbird expert, René Primevère Lesson, using the name* sasin; *Allen did not make the distinction between the two species until fifty years later.*

Below: The Green-backed Firecrown migrates farther south than any other hummingbird. It breeds in Tierra del Fuego at the tip of Argentina.

19

*This is a curious illustration because it shows
a male Broad-tailed Hummingbird with a
nest. It is odd because male hummingbirds
take no part in nest building, brooding, or
rearing the young.*

All these descriptions created in Europe a vast hunger to see these tiny wonders. Hundreds upon hundreds of hummingbirds were caught, killed, and sent back to kings, popes, princes, scientists, museum curators, and collectors of curiosities. Feathers, skins, nests, and eggs were also collected and sent back to the Old World. Many of these items never reached their destinations. The Honorable John Winthrop, Governor of Connecticut, wrote the English naturalist Francis Willughby in October 1670 of a "curiously contrived Nest of the Humming Bird" lost when "the Vessel miscarrying, you received them not." Virginia colonist and collector John Bannister bewailed the loss of a female Ruby-throated Hummingbird skin to hungry cockroaches. Europe paid well for the colonists' trouble: A single preserved hummingbird skin could sell for as much as eight pounds sterling.

As trade increased between the Old and New Worlds, hummingbird feathers were much in demand. Milliners wanted them to decorate ladies' hats, dressmakers wanted them to adorn dresses—craftsmen of all sorts wanted them for their work. Numerous authorities report that untold millions of preserved hummingbird skins were shipped to London and Paris from Santa Fe de Bogotá, Rio de Janeiro, and other South American ports. A single shipment from one Brazilian port consisted of three thousand skins of the Ruby-topaz Hummingbird *(Orthoryncus mosquitus).* On March 21, 1888, at one sale in London, more than twelve thousand hummingbird skins were sold, and thousands more were auctioned off a few weeks later. In one year, one London dealer imported four hundred thousand hummingbird skins from the West Indies alone. A single hummingbird skin might be sold in London for anywhere from a mere two shillings to as much as two hundred shillings, depending on the rarity and beauty of the hummingbird.

No one knows exactly how many hummingbirds were destroyed to supply the European market, for the numbers received in Europe were but a portion of those killed. Many skins were spoiled in the process of capture, many others were destroyed by tropical insects that dined on them, ruined by moisture and mildew, lost on the long journeys overland to shipping ports, and many more vanished with ships lost at sea. The trading of hummingbird skins went on at a feverish pace for more than a hundred years. No one can say with absolute certainty that the trade brought any given hummingbird species to extinction, but there are some species that are known to science only from the old trade skins. These species have not been reported in their native haunts during this century.

By sad coincidence, the booming market for hummingbird skins came at the same time that scientists were struggling to establish an orderly method for identifying living creatures, animals, and plants alike. Linnaeus had introduced the Latin binomial approach to taxonomy, and scientists of the 1700s and 1800s were wrestling valiantly to classify the hummingbirds and to clarify the confusion that inevitably surrounds a family with hundreds of different species. It is impossible to guess how many hummingbird species were eliminated before they were even identified, how many species were made

The Broad-tailed Hummingbird is found in the Rocky Mountains and the Great Basin Mountains in North America. Its Latin name, Selasphorus platycercus, *means "flat-tailed torchbearer." The shape, color, and pattern of various tail feathers are the ways ornithologists identify difficult hummingbirds. This is a male Broad-tailed Hummingbird, which is fairly uncomplicated to identify; the female is more challenging since it is easily confused with Rufous, Allen's, and Calliope females (not to mention that immatures of these four species all tend to look like females).*

Opposite page: Hummingbird kachinas like these and hummingbirds themselves were both called Tocha *by the Hopi Indians. The Zunis called them* Tanya. *The Hopis and Zunis believed that hummingbirds brought the rain, and hummingbird rain dances were done in hopes of enticing rain to the desert. Kachinas were used in hummingbird dances and ceremonies in which the dancers wore masks with long bills, green feathers on their arms, turquoise and silver necklaces and bracelets, elaborate knee-length skirts trimmed with foxtails, circlets of bells at each knee, and boots with bells and tassels.*

Below: Some hummingbirds have magnificent crests and ear tufts, as does this Tufted Coquette. Others have amazingly long or strangely shaped tails, puffs of feathers on their legs, or bills like Turkish scimitars.

extinct by human curiosity and avarice, condemned by human carelessness to disappear without so much as a name to mark their existence on the earth.

However, the business of killing hummingbirds was by no means an innovation of the conquistadors and colonists. The native peoples of South and Central America had long believed that hummingbirds were magical, and collected them for their magic powers. Hummingbird bodies were, and still are, considered particularly potent love charms, guaranteed to draw one's beloved simply by holding it in one's hand or carrying it in one's pocket.

Native markets in Mexico that specialize in selling magic potions, healing herbs, and love amulets still feature coffee cans stuffed with the battered and bedraggled bodies of dried hummingbirds. The more affluent can purchase them prepackaged in red silk drawstring bags, complete with printed prayers to lure a lover. For those who perceive a connection between personal cleanliness and love, there is a "miraculous hummingbird soap," the use of which in one's ablutions assures one of "attracting, conquering, and dominating" the loved one (assuming, of course, that the purchaser believes that conquering and dominating have anything to do with love).

Little bags of powdered hummingbirds are still sold door to door as love potions by rural pedlars in Mexico, and they are by no means inexpensive: $80 is the average price, more than a month's income for many families. And, of course, hummingbirds stuffed and mounted are also available.

The hummingbird featured as largely in Native North American myth as it did in magic. It starred in both the stories of Creation and those of the Great Flood. In the Amerindian version of the Great Flood, the hummingbird was sent to see if the waters had subsided from the land, as the dove was in the Bible (Genesis 8: 8–12). One of the most powerful *kachina* spirits (small wooden figures carved to represent the spirits of the Hopi religion) was Tocha, the hummingbird.

The Navaho ranked the hummingbird as one of the four bravest creatures they knew, the four creatures that had gone to a mystic land to find food for the Navaho in a time of terrible famine. The white wolf returned with white corn, the mountain lion with yellow corn, the bluebird with blue corn, and the hummingbird returned with an ear of corn of many colors — red, white, blue, and yellow — the colors of its own bright feathers.

It is odd how remnants of these legends still touch our lives today. Where I live in northern California, it is customary to hang several ears of multi-colored Indian corn on the door at Thanksgiving, an obvious reference to the Navaho's gratitude for receiving the gift of food in a time of famine. But in all the years I'd hung the brightly colored corn, I never knew that it was the gift of the hummingbird.

Whenever hummingbirds were found in semi-arid lands — the southwestern United States, central Mexico, the coastal deserts of Peru — the native peoples have associated them with life-giving rain. The Pimas, Hopis, Zuni, and other Pueblo Indians believed that the hummingbirds could intercede with the Great Spirit to bring rain when necessary. Water jars frequently bore the likeness of rainbirds, some too stylized to identify, others that are unmistakably hummingbirds. The Nazca people of Peru, best known for their huge desert drawings that gain perspective only when seen from the air, also painted hummingbirds on their water jars, an invocation, as it were, that the jars might be well filled. The Hopi and Zuni tribes called the hummingbird the "Rain Bringer," and the kachina rain dances were often danced by children — a small nod to hummingbirds' diminutive size. Miniature Tocha kachinas were given out to the children of the tribe after the rain dance, that they might know and remember their tribal traditions.

These native peoples associated hummingbirds and rain because the rain, especially in dry country, brings flowers. Hummingbirds cannot live without the nectar of the flowers, and part of the ecological role they play is that of pollinators. The rain brought the flowers, which brought the hummingbirds, but the natives seeing all three at once, believed that hummingbirds brought rain.

Opposite page: John Gould, Britain's most famous trochilidist (hummingbird expert), published a monograph on hummingbirds accompanied by magnificent illustrations between 1849 and 1861, with additional supplements published between 1880 and 1885. Gould's superb watercolors are now as prized by art collectors as they have been by ornithologists and naturalists for over one hundred years.

Above: This Apache dancer's mask depicts a hummingbird in flight. The dance symbolized the warrior's desire to be swift-footed and hard to see like the hummingbird, which flies very fast and is difficult to see in flight.

Opposite page: The White-tipped Sickle-bill is specifically adapted to feeding from heliconia flowers. These tubular, yellow flowers enclosed by thick, furry, red bracts have a curvature that is matched precisely by the beak of the Sicklebill.

Below: In 1829, The Anna's Humming-bird was named for Anne de Belle Massena (1806–1896), Duchess of Rivoli, who was described by John James Audubon as "a beautiful young woman, not more than twenty, extremely graceful and polite." Anne was the wife of François Victor Massena (1798–1863), Duke of Rivoli and Prince of Essling, a marshal of France under Napoleon. Together the Duke and Duchess sponsored numerous ornithological expeditions to increase their collection of hummingbird skins. The Rivoli Hummingbird was named after the Duke in 1827, but the English name was changed to the Magnificent Hummingbird in 1983.

Certainly, hummingbirds love water, and they also appear to like to play a lot. There are areas of my garden that must be watered by hand; one area is very close to a hawthorn tree that I have long suspected of harboring a hummingbird nest, although in all my years of peering into its thickety branches I've never found it. Yet when I water my garden, the spray from the hose arches up into the air, and the Anna's Hummingbird that I believe lives in the hawthorn comes out and does dives and rolls through the spray that the navy's Blue Angels would envy for speed and skill. It has not been proven that the hummingbird likes to play in the spray, but that Anna's Hummingbird darts and dashes through the water with sufficient regularity that on those occasions when it has more compelling business, I am disappointed that it isn't there, flying faster than I can make out its form, throwing flashes of red and green from all angles.

Rufous-tailed Hummingbirds *(Amazilia tzacatl)* have been observed sliding down banana leaves spangled with raindrops or dew. The Violet-bellied Hummingbird *(Damophila julie)* will skim over a pool in a jungle stream, half-immerse itself, and fly to a nearby twig to complete its toilette, shaking the water out of its plumage, and preening. Dr. Alexander Skutch relates the story of an Anna's Hummingbird that discovered that she could ride the stream of water from a hose, perching on it like a branch and riding it forward through the air. She repeated the trick over and over, apparently enjoying herself thoroughly.

Hummingbirds, like bees and butterflies, pollinate flowers. They are brushed with pollen in the process of feeding and carry it to the next flower at which they feed. In Central and South America, hummingbirds pollinate many different kinds of orchids, including the orchid from which vanilla is made. The secret of growing vanilla was closely guarded for three hundred years until some French planters smuggled vanilla cuttings to Bourbon Island in the Indian Ocean. The vanilla grew, but it never produced the seedpods from which vanilla is made because Bourbon Island had no hummingbirds to pollinate the flowers (hummingbirds are found only in the Americas). The French had to pollinate the orchids by hand with a splinter of bamboo the size and shape of a hummingbird beak.

The hummingbird's swiftness gave it an important part in many Amerindian legends: Whenever an important task had to be carried out at top speed, the hummingbird was chosen to do it. In Native American stories, the hummingbird, spectacularly handsome and infinitely bold, is always portrayed as the most desirable suitor of all.

In the Caribbean, the Arawaks and Warraus called the hummingbird the "doctor bird" because it played a prominent role in the rituals of their medicine men. Three of the four species of hummingbird found in Jamaica today are known as doctor birds: The Jamaican Mango *(Anthracothorax dominicus)* is the Doctor Bird, the Vervain Hummingbird *(Mellisuga minima)* is the Little Doctor Bird, and the Streamertail *(Trochilus polytmus)* is the Long-tailed Doctor Bird.

On a trip to Jamaica a few years ago, I stayed in Negril. A friend had told me that the one thing I absolutely must do, without fail, was go to Rick's Café to watch the sun set over the Caribbean from the Café's patio on a high cliff above the sea. I promised faithfully to do so, and every night for nearly three weeks I tried. But every night on my way there, I was stopped in my tracks by a huge hibiscus hedge where dozens of all four species of Jamaican hummingbird fed at dusk. I was familiar with Anna's, Costa's *(Archilochus costae)*, and Rufous Hummingbirds from California, and with Black-fronted Hummingbirds *(Hylocharis xantusii)* from Cabo San Lucas in Baja California, but I felt as though I had never seen a hummingbird until I saw the Streamertail. It has a metallic green, blue, and yellow body; it has a black cap and a black-tipped red bill; and it has a flamboyant black tail 6–7 inches (15–17.5 cm) long, far longer than its body. I was enchanted. In the three weeks I was in Negril I never once got to Rick's Café in time to watch the sun set. Instead, I watched these glorious hummingbirds dart and dash, creating flashes of color as they fed on red and yellow hibiscus until it was too dark to see them anymore.

The Streamertail is called the Long-tailed Doctor Bird in Jamaica, where it is the official national bird. Having these birds feed from your hand at Lisa Salmon's Bird Feeding Station, a few miles outside Montego Bay, Jamaica, is a delightful and extraordinary experience.

HUMMINGBIRD ANATOMY

Size

Hummingbirds are the smallest of all the 8,700 species of birds known to live on earth. The Bee Hummingbird *(Mellisuga helenae)* of Cuba is the smallest and weighs less than a penny (.07 ounces or 2 g) and at 2¼ inches (5.5 cm) long, is smaller than most people's thumbs. The largest hummingbird, the Giant Hummingbird *(Patagonia gigas)*, is a giant only when measured against other hummingbirds; it is actually about the size of a barn swallow, 8½ inches (21 cm) long, and weighs about .7 ounces (20 g). The smallest bird in North America is the Calliope Hummingbird *(Stellula calliope)*, 3 inches (7.5 cm) long. It would take ten Calliopes to weigh as much as a first-class letter (each weighs .1 ounce or 3 g).

Bills and Tongues

Besides their tiny size, hummingbirds are most easily identified by their long, delicately slender bills. Hummingbird bills may be straight, as most are, or curved either upward or downward. The longest hummingbird bill belongs to the Sword-billed Hummingbird *(Ensifera ensifera)*, which, at 4 inches (10 cm) is longer than the rest of the bird, body and tail together. The Purple-backed Thornbill *(Ramphomicron microrhynchum)* has the stubbiest bill, scarcely ⁵/₁₆ inches (.8 cm), not even as long as its head.

Hummingbirds' bills may be black, red, or yellow, or a combination of colors, such as red tipped with black. Most bills are dark colored, but, of the North American species, the Berylline *(Amazilia beryllina)*, Broad-billed *(Cynanthus latirostis)*, Buff-bellied *(Phaethornus subochraceus)*, Violet-crowned *(Amazilia violiceps)*, and White-eared *(Cynanthus Basilinna leucotis)* have red or mostly red beaks. The beaks of the species seen in North America don't have the diversity of shape as those of their South American cousins.

Opposite page: The Broad-billed Hummingbird was first classified in 1827 by the British naturalist William Swainson. Its scientific name, Cynanthus latirostris, *means "bright blue broad bill," which describes the beak and the peacock-blue gorget of males like this one. In Mexico, the Broad-billed Hummingbird is called* la matraquita, *"the little rattle shaker," because it makes sounds like the rattles shaken during rain dance ceremonies.*

Below: The Calliope Hummingbird is the smallest hummingbird found in North America.

Right: The White-tipped Sicklebill perches to feed instead of hovering like most hummingbirds do. It is found from Costa Rica to Peru and feeds on wild plantain. Hummingbirds such as the Sicklebill have bills specifically adapted to particular flowers and get the nectar they need by repeated visits to those flowers; they do not defend a territory as do hummingbirds that forage at many different types of flowers.

Above: This White-tailed Starfrontlet is cleaning its bill with its feet. Hummingbirds use their feet to cling to perches, scratch themselves, and clean their bills. They'd much rather fly than walk or even hop. The White-tailed Starfrontlet is found only in Colombia.

The variety of shapes of southern hummingbirds' bills are suggested by their names: Saw-billed Hermit *(Ramphodon naevius)*, Hook-billed Hermit *(Ramphodon dohrnii)*, and Green-fronted Lancebill *(Doryfera ludoviciae)*. Some beaks curve upward like those of the Fiery-tailed Awlbill *(Avocettula recurvirostris)* and Mountain Avocetbill *(Opisthoprora euryptera)*, and others curve downward as sharply as a Turkish scimitar, like the bill of the White-tipped Sicklebill *(Eutoxeres aquila)*. Different bills serve different purposes. The White-tipped Sicklebill is adapted to perching and probing heliconia blossoms; the Sword-billed Hummingbird uses its 4-inch (10-cm) beak to get to the nectar of species like the huge pendant trumpets of the arborescent angel's trumpet *(Brugmansia candida, Brugmansia sanguinea* and spp.). The flowers of this tree are so huge that their nectar is well beyond the reach of most birds and insects; each flower is 8 to 10 inches (20–25 cm) long, and so wide that the hummingbird can fly right into it. In the process of feeding, of course, the birds are dusted with pollen, which they carry from flower to flower.

Hummingbirds have a remarkable number of uses for their bills. The bill is a feeding tube, protective casing for the tongue, and a dueling weapon. Hummingbirds also use their beaks much in the same way humans use their hands; the birds use their beaks to fetch and carry nesting material, weave amazingly intricate and nearly invisible nests, preen themselves, and feed themselves and their young. They also use their beaks as formidable weapons. Coupled with the birds' reckless courage (or pugnacity) and agility, the bills enable them to attack and drive off birds many times their size—even the mightiest predators of the bird kingdom, owls, eagles, and hawks. The bill is too delicate to actually stab with, but as a threat it is sufficiently effective.

Most often, though, hummingbirds use their beaks to spar with each other. At Lisa Salmon's Bird Feeding Station a few miles outside Montego Bay, Jamaica (the Jamaican government insists in calling the station a bird sanctuary; Ms. Salmon insists it is not), one can sit in the arbor, hold small bottles of sugar water, and watch hummingbirds feed only an arm's length away. Of course, this occurs only when the birds are not busy driving each other off. They zoom at each other like *Star Wars'* fighter planes, flashing brilliant colors as they fly in every direction. But when the game gets dull, they settle down to refuel in flight at the hand-held feeders.

The hummingbird bill is also magnificently adapted to the bird's role as a flower-feeder and pollinator. Ornithologists were puzzled for years as to how the bill worked. How, exactly, did hummingbirds manage to refuel on the wing? Did hummingbirds suck the nectar through their bills like a straw? Did they survive on nothing but flower nectar? Could they possibly catch insects on the wing with such tiny mouths?

In fact, the bill only provides the hummingbird with access to the flower: The bird's long white tongue licks the nectar at a rate of thirteen licks per second, and draws it up by capillary action. The bird swallows the nectar when it pulls its tongue back into its beak. The number of licks does not vary with the size of the hummingbird, but the bigger the bird is, the bigger its tongue — larger birds get more nectar per lick. A hummingbird can lick anywhere from .1 to .3 ounces (3–8 g) of nectar from a feeder at a time.

Pages 36–37: Broad-billed Hummingbirds breed in southern Arizona, southwestern New Mexico, and western Texas, where they often feed from cactus flowers like those on the claret cup cactus (Echinocereus triglochidiatus). Hummingbirds are especially attracted to red flowers because they do not have to compete with bees for the nectar; bees cannot see the color red, and hummingbirds can. Hummingbirds rely on vision to find nectar-rich flowers, while bees use smell; hummingbirds are attracted by color, bees by fragrance. The nectar of tubular flowers can be reached easily by hummingbirds with their long beaks and longer tongues, but is less accessible to bees.

Below: The Copper-rumped Hummingbird is native to Venezuela, Trinidad, and Tobago. It feeds from, and pollinates, tobacco. The Arawak Indians of the South American mainland raided Trinidad to get cultivated tobacco, which they regarded as a powerful medicine. They called the hummingbirds, whose cross-pollination assured good crops, "Medicine Birds" or "Doctor Birds."

Like its beak, the hummingbird's tongue is a remarkable organ. Divided in two at the tip, it is grooved halfway up the middle; these tips help the hummingbird catch tiny flower mites and spiders hidden deep in flowers. The tongue is fringed along the edges, and the bird can roll each side into a tube, but since it has been demonstrated that hummingbirds don't suck nectar, no one knows quite what purpose this ability serves. The tongue is much larger than the bill, which is why the bird can stick its tongue out to lick nectar. The back portion of the tongue wraps back around the skull on a forked bone, and is anchored at the middle of the forehead between the eyes.

Hummingbirds have forty to sixty taste buds, unlike people, who have about ten thousand, and only a few are located on the tongue. The majority are found in the back of the mouth on the soft palate, under the tongue, and near the larynx. There are enough taste buds on their tongues for hummingbirds to determine the sweetness of nectar and feeding solutions. They prefer a solution of four parts water to one part sugar, and will refuse solutions that are only half as sweet (8:1).

Diet and Metabolism

While it may be logical to think that insect-eating birds should have wide gapes, since most of the insectivorous birds, like flycatchers, do, hummingbirds do not. Tiny insects are an important part of their diet. In fact, they have been observed diving like hawks into swarms of insects. They catch flies, ants, small beetles, and tiny wasps, and are not above helping themselves to bugs caught in a spider's web, and to the spider, too.

Sweet sap is also on some hummingbirds' menus, but since they cannot drill with their beaks, they sneak in for a lick at wells drilled by sapsuckers. In the Rocky Mountains, Rufous and Broad-tailed Hummingbirds partake of sweet sap at wells drilled by red-naped sapsuckers. East of the Rockies, Ruby-throated Hummingbirds have a lick on the fly at wells drilled by downy woodpeckers and yellow-bellied sapsuckers. Michigan researchers William Foster and James Tate observed that Ruby-throated Hummingbirds visited the sap pits of yellow-bellied sapsuckers more often than the sapsuckers themselves. In tropical forests, hummingbirds sometimes sip the juices of sweet, ripe fruit.

The early collectors believed that hummingbirds needed only nectar; consequently, there were many failed attempts to keep the birds in captivity, both by private collectors and zoos. The first live hummingbird to arrive in Europe was a Sparkling Violet-ear (*Colibri coruscans*), which arrived at the Zoological Gardens in Regent's Park in London on November 25, 1905. For fourteen days the bird enchanted all who saw it. Then it died because nobody knew what to feed it, although it was offered a wide variety of foods.

Page 39, top and bottom: Hummingbirds often eat more than half their total body weight in food every day, and they drink eight times their weight in water every day. They feed from five to eight times an hour, and even more frequently than that just after dawn and just before dusk. These Broad-tailed Hummingbirds are feeding on honeysuckle nectar.

© Derek Fell

Above: Trumpet honeysuckle (Lonicera sempervirens) is a perfect ornithophilous (hummingbird-pollinated) flower: showy, red to orange, unscented, trumpet-shaped, day-blooming, and nectar-rich.

Many solutions were offered to captive hummingbirds before it was discovered what they liked to eat. The solutions were often mixtures of various ingredients: honey, sugar, water, vitamins, condensed milk, meat extract, fresh ant pupae, egg yolk, mealworms, carrots, peeled grapes, horse liver, horse heart, veal, baby food, grasshoppers, seaweed meal, apples, oranges, bananas, lettuce leaves, calcium, dried shrimp, sprouted wheat, silkworm pupae, rusk meal, and Nestlé's milk. Frankly, it's a wonder any captive hummingbirds ate at all!

Finally, more than fifty years later, the German ornithologist Walter Scheithauer worked out a reasonably balanced diet of a 4:1 water-and-sugar solution combined with swarms of free-flying fruit flies *(Drosophila)* on which hummingbirds could be kept in captivity in relatively good health. Today, the ecological perception militates strongly against keeping hummingbirds—or any wild creature—in captivity.

Hummingbirds have taken warm-blooded miniaturization just about as far as it can go. Larger animals have proportionately less surface area to lose heat, which makes it possible for them to have a slower metabolism and still maintain a high body temperature. If hummingbirds were any smaller, they would not be able to eat fast enough to stay alive.

Hummingbirds must metabolize food with extraordinary rapidity. In general, they feed five to eight times an hour, and Rufous Hummingbirds have been observed feeding fifteen times an hour—about every four minutes. The birds feed most heavily in the morning and again at dusk. In order to process food fast enough, the stomach digests mostly insects; nectar appears to bypass the stomach and proceed directly to the intestine for immediate absorption into the bloodstream. Almost 100 percent of the sugar consumed by hummingbirds is absorbed into the body, a higher rate of food absorption than is currently known for any other bird. Hummingbirds can digest a bellyful of insects in as little as ten minutes.

This is not to suggest that hummingbirds do not eat much. They eat half their weight in food a day, the equivalent of a 150-pound (67.5-kg) person eating 75 pounds (34 kg) of food a day. For a human to maintain the same weight/metabolism ratio as a hummingbird, a 150-pound (67.5-kg) person would have to eat 300 pounds (135 kg) of food a day. That person would require 155,000 calories a day, and their temperature would be 750°F (399°C). Normal consumption for a human adult is between 2 and 2½ pounds (.9–1 kg) of food per day, or 2,500 calories, and normal human temperature is 98.6°F (37°C).

If eating half their weight in food a day sounds amazing, consider the fact that hummingbirds drink eight times their weight in water each day. A 150-pound (67.5-kg) person would have to drink 150 gallons (570 l) of water a day to take in an equivalent amount of liquid. (A gallon [3.8 l] of water weighs 8 pounds [3.6 kg].)

Opposite page: Hummingbirds lick nectar from flowers, as these Antillean Hummingbirds are doing.

Hummingbirds must learn which flowers have sufficient nectar of sufficient sweetness to make the caloric expenditure of hovering worthwhile. They learn from their mothers, who teach them which flowers to feed from and how to get the nectar. Mother hummingbirds have been seen teaching young birds how to use a feeder as well. A Broadtailed Hummingbird feeds from a thistle, below, while the Streamertail, bottom, finds sustenance in one of Jamaica's bright tropical flowers.

Hummingbirds' energy needs range from 6,660 to 12,400 calories per day. A hovering 3- to 4-ounce (84–112-g) hummingbird uses 35 calories per minute; by comparison, a bumblebee uses only $\frac{1}{2}$ calorie per minute. One analysis of caloric expenditure for a wild Anna's Hummingbird on an average day showed that it spent 3,810 calories perching, 90 chasing insects, 2,460 drinking nectar, and 300 defending its territory —a total of 6,660 calories. To get 6,660 calories from the nectar of fuchsias alone would require feeding from more than 1,000 fuchsia blossoms.

Hummingbirds must learn which flowers contain enough nectar to make expending the energy required to hover long enough to get the nectar worthwhile. They do not know this instinctively, but learn by trial and error. Hummingbirds have little sense of smell, so fragrance does not help them find flowers or choose which flowers to feed from. They use their eyes to find the flowers, and their tongues to determine if there is enough nectar of sufficient sweetness to eat. The amount of sugar in the nectar is what determines whether the bird will return to the flower, not color or structure.

It is commonly believed that hummingbirds are attracted to red tubular flowers, but the fact is that hummingbirds are attracted to any flower that has a lot of nectar. Hummingbirds are attracted to flowers that: (1) offer nectar of sufficient sweetness; (2) are spaced far enough apart that the bird can hover without hitting its wings; and (3) spare them a great deal of competition with bees. It is true that hummingbirds compete less with bees when feeding on tubular flowers because the bees cannot crawl down to the nectar easily; it is also true that many of the flowers that meet these criteria are red. There are 129 species of hummingbird-pollinated wildflowers in the southwestern United States, 20 in the northeast, 80 in California, 50 in Arizona, 40 in New Mexico, 28 in Oregon, 19 in Colorado, 14 in Idaho, 10 in the southern half of British Columbia, and 5 in Alaska. In addition, there are many more garden flowers from which hummingbirds feed. (See page 130.)

On January 26, 1827, the French naval vessel Heros, *under the command of Captain August Duhaut-Cilly, lay at anchor in San Francisco Bay, California. The captain and Dr. Paul Emile Botta, the ship's physician and naturalist, were invited by Padre Tomas of the Mission Dolores to see a most unusual hummingbird, a hummingbird that did not migrate. The captain's log entry for that date reads: "It has head and throat of glowing fire.... When the bewitching creature alights upon a bare branch, for some short seconds, one would say it was a ruby spheroid, or rather a little ball of red-hot iron giving off a shower of sparks. When several are seen together on the same branch, anyone versed in the marvels of Araby might imagine it a wand set with precious gems...." The eloquent captain had just seen an Anna's hummingbird.*

Hummingbirds also do not take kindly to finding a lack of food where they are accustomed to finding plenty. I used to work in an old-fashioned sun-room where a hummingbird feeder hung from the eaves. I always knew when the feeder was empty because the Anna's Hummingbird that lived in my hawthorn tree would hover beside the feeder, squeak furiously, then come to the window nearest my desk to squeak at me personally. The bird would dart back and forth between the inexcusably empty feeder and me, complaining bitterly until I got up and filled it.

Brain, Heart, and Lungs

Hummingbirds have one of the largest brains, relative to their size, of all birds. The brain comprises 4.2 percent of the hummingbird's total body weight.

Likewise, hummingbirds have large hearts. In fact, they have proportionally the largest hearts of any living animal. The heart constitutes from 1.75 to 2.5 percent of their total body weight, the equivalent of a 150-pound (67.5-kg) person having a heart weighing 3 to 4 pounds (1–2 kg). Smaller hummingbirds have proportionally larger hearts than bigger hummingbirds in order to maintain the extraordinary metabolic rate required for feeding while flying and to maintain their normal body temperature of about 105°F (40°C). Resting heartbeat for a Blue-throated Hummingbird (*Lampornis clemenciae*) is 480 beats per minute, and it can go as high as 1,260 beats per second when the bird is excited.

Hummingbirds are in flight before they release their hold on their perch, as this Purple-throated Carib demonstrates. By the time they let go, their wings are close to full flight speed.

It takes a lot of oxygen to fuel the fires of hummingbird metabolism. Just as their hearts are outsized, so are their lungs and air passages. Resting hummingbirds breathe 250 times per minute; in moments of excitement, the rate goes up to 273 times per minute. By comparison, people normally breathe 16 times per minute. Research shows that hummingbirds use eight times as much oxygen as songbirds. One study done of five different species of hummingbirds indicated that on an hourly basis, the birds consumed oxygen at rates ranging from 2.5 to 8.8 cubic inches (42–147 cm³) per .3 ounce (1 g) of body weight. To translate this into human terms, a 150-pound (68-kg) person would need from 1,500–52,800 cubic feet (45–1,584 cm³) of oxygen per hour. Hummingbirds use seven times more oxygen when hovering than when perched.

The lungs of the hummingbird are large in proportion to the size of the bird, but small in terms of absolute size. To supplement the lungs' air capacity, hummingbirds have nine air sacs tucked into all the spaces not occupied by their other organs. Scientists speculate that the air sacs help the bird regulate its temperature by cooling it off when it gets too warm. Birds have no sweat glands, and as anyone who has ever worn a down jacket knows, feathers are superb at holding heat. Other than the air sacs, the hummingbird's only method of cooling off is to pant heavily, pulling fresher, cooler air into its internal evaporative system.

Torpor

Hummingbirds are the only birds that regularly become torpid at night. Their normal temperature of 105°F (40°C) can drop to 66.2°F (19°C), or nearly half. If a human being's temperature were to drop from the normal 98.6°F (37°C) to 49.3°F (9.6°C), the person would die. Torpid hummingbirds are still and stiff as corpses and cannot fly, although they may squeak if pried loose from the branches they cling to tightly with their feet. Because so many hummingbird species are found along the equator, the popular impression is that they are creatures of warm climates and lowland jungles. The fact is that more hummingbird species are native to the high Andes, with its extreme temperatures and bitterly cold nights typical of high altitudes, than to the tropical rain forests of the Amazon.

Dr. Augusto Ruschi, of Santa Theresa, Espírito Santo, in southern Brazil was one of the first to keep hummingbirds in captivity successfully. He had huge aviaries 150 feet (45 m) long, 45 feet (13.5 m) wide, and 18 feet (5.4 m) high. The aviaries were heavily planted with flowering eucalypts *(Eucalyptus* spp.*)* covered with epiphytic orchids *(Orchidaceae* spp.*)* and bromeliads *(Bromeliaceae* spp.*)* as well as shrubs like hibiscus *(Hibiscus* spp.*)* Outside the aviaries, in a huge parkland planted with eucalyptus trees, the air swarmed with wild hummingbirds. According to Walter Scheithauer, the German ornithologist, one could sometimes see more than one hundred hummingbirds in one tree, representing as many as fourteen different species. In addition to the natural nectar from the flowers, Ruschi supplemented the caged birds' diet with sugar water and masses of fruit flies attracted by rotting fruit in the aviaries. At feeders hung from the veranda of the house it was possible to see thirty-two different species over the period of a year. Ruschi found that some of the hummingbirds in his aviary went into torpidity (noctivated) almost every night, and others did so no more than twice a week. Some noctivated from eight to fourteen hours when the weather was cool, not rousing from their torpor until the sun had dissipated the chill of the morning. By contrast, some North American hummingbirds emerge from torpor before dawn, apparently in response to their own internal rhythm.

It takes a while for hummingbirds to come out of their torpor. Ruschi's birds could be held in the hand for an hour before they were fully roused to activity. Torpid Anna's and Allen's Hummingbirds roused in the middle of the night could fly reasonably well after ten or fifteen minutes. Hummingbirds cannot fly until their temperature returns to at least 86°F (30°C).

The amount of energy hummingbirds actually save by becoming torpid is determined by the air temperature and wind chill factor. The metabolism of a sleeping hummingbird decreases when the weather is warm because it doesn't need to generate as much energy to keep itself warm. The temperature of a torpid bird increases as external temperatures rise, exactly like that of a lizard on a warm rock. At 60°F (15.6°C), a noctivating bird

Hummingbirds are the only birds that become regularly torpid at night.

expends only one-fiftieth or one-sixtieth of the energy it would usually need to maintain its body temperature.

In the high Andes, where many hummingbird species live, the temperature often drops below freezing at night. In addition, rain, hail, or snow during the day limits the hummingbirds' feeding time. The hummingbirds must go torpid at night to keep from freezing to death. Roosting or nesting in the open would expend too much energy, since body heat would escape to the open sky. Some South American species, such as the Andean Hillstar *(Oreotrochilus estella)* sleep in caves or abandoned mine shafts where the temperature at night stays a few degrees above freezing, and less energy is lost to radiation.

Ordinarily the old proverb "Birds of a feather stick together" is true. However, hummingbirds do not roost together for warmth like other birds. But they do share their caves in the Andes with other species: flycatchers, finches, ovenbirds, geese, and even hawks and owls. The only known instance of colonial nesting among hummingbirds was found in a shallow cave in the wall of a deep ravine on Cotopaxi, where the weather just below the great ice cap that covers the top of the mountain is notoriously nasty. At these elevations (13,000 to 15,000 feet [3,900–4,500 m]), gale-force winds, heavy rains, snow, and night temperatures below freezing are common. In the cave, scientist Corley Smith found five occupied Andean Hillstar nests within a radius of 7 feet (2 m).

In the past, ornithologists did not believe native tales of birds that hibernated, but time and scientific research has proved the First Peoples right. It is now recognized that the poorwills of the American West sometimes hibernate for months. Several species of swifts and African mousebirds (colies) also become torpid when the weather is cold. To understand the energy savings achieved by torpidity, it helps to know the differences between the energy expenditure required for flight, normal rest, and torpidity. The heart of the Blue-throated Hummingbird beats 1,260 times per minute when it is flying, and 480 times per minute when resting quietly, and only 36 times per minute when it is torpid.

Longevity

Hummingbirds epitomize Type-A behavior so perfectly that one would assume that they would burn themselves out very quickly, but that does not seem to be the case at all. In Dr. Ruschi's aviary, the average life span was ten years. There are reports of a Planalto Hermit *(Phaethornis pretrei)* that was still going strong after fourteen years, and some free-living hummingbirds near Dr. Ruschi's home were alive nine years after being banded. A Green-throated Carib *(Sericotes holosericeus)*, an adult when it came to live in the Jewel Room at the Bronx Zoo, lived another ten and one-half years, and a Purple-throated Carib *(Eulampis jugularis)* delighted visitors there for nearly ten years. The fact

Once the hummingbird's diet was understood to be a combination of nectar and insects, survival rates in captivity improved tremendously. Hummingbirds have lived from ten to fourteen years in captivity. At zoos all over the world the hummingbird aviary is called the Jewel Room.

that many species have been observed building nests in the same place, one on top of the other, year after year, suggests that hummingbirds may live from five to ten years or more in the wild.

Sleep

Hummingbirds don't sleep like other birds, with their heads tucked under their wings. Instead they roost with their necks pulled down, heads out, and bills pointed up in the air. Most small birds prefer to sleep in some hidden place, well concealed from predators, yet Dr. Alexander Skutch, an American ornithologist who lives in Costa Rica, tells of frequently finding Long-billed Starthroats *(Heliomaster longirostris)* roosting on the topmost twig of a tall tree, "as conspicuous against the sky as such a small bird can be." Scaly-breasted Hummingbirds *(Phaeochroa cuvierii)* settle down for the night by twitching their heads from side to side, sometimes for fifteen minutes before finally dropping off to sleep, bill pointed upward, defying the sky.

Eyes

The Black-breasted Plovercrest is native to South America, and is found from Brazil to Argentina. Of the 338 different species of hummingbirds, 299 breed in Central and South America, 16 in North America and 15 in the Caribbean. For 8 species, the range is not yet known.

Hummingbirds' eyes are immobile, unlike human eyes. Their huge, bright, black eyes are placed on the sides of their heads. To see from side to side, hummingbirds must move their heads from side to side. They have both monocular and binocular vision, which means they can see both to the side and forward. Humans have only binocular

vision: Images from each eye are fused into a single image in the brain so we don't see double. Because the human eye moves, there is some peripheral vision, but not nearly as much as we would have if our eyes were placed above our ears instead of above our noses. Hummingbirds' eyes are located quite high on the head, possibly to help them see predators striking from above, such as hawks.

In proportion to their size, birds have much larger eyes than mammals; both eyes typically outweigh the brain. Like other birds, reptiles, and seals, hummingbirds have a third eyelid, the nictitating membrane. It is transparent, and moistens and cleans the cornea in addition to protecting the eye.

Not all birds' eyes are the same shape. Owls have flat eyes; swans have tubular eyes; and hummingbirds have round eyes. Hummingbirds' eyes are .2 to .3 inches (6–8 mm) in diameter. Hummingbirds have two areas in their retinas that allow them to focus very closely. The fovea centralis focuses sharply to the side. Scientists call it the "search" fovea on the theory that it allows the hummingbird to distinguish objects in green areas, such as individual leaves and flowers on trees and shrubs. The fovea temporalis allows the bird to focus closely when it is using its binocular vision to look straight head. Scientists call it the "pursuit" fovea, on the theory that it helps the hummingbird spot and pursue insects in flight.

Hummingbirds cannot move their eyes. Unlike humans, they have no peripheral vision. To see from side to side, they must move their heads. Human beings have binocular vision, but hummingbirds have both binocular and monocular vision. Imagine having eyes on the sides of your head and being able to focus each eye independently — that's monocular vision. It means that the bird's brain can interpret two independent images simultaneously. The human brain fuses the two images received from each eye into a single image — that's binocular vision, and hummingbirds have that, too. This Frilled Coquette has its head tilted enough to suggest that it's using monocular vision.

Feathers: Crests, Tails, and Iridescence

Opposite page: The iridescent gorget of the male hummingbird must be at the right angle to the sun to flash this glorious, glittering color. In addition, the viewer must be standing at the right angle to see the color. Color is produced either by pigment or structure. Pigmented colors look the same from all angles; structural colors depend on the angle of light in relation to the angle of the viewer. Iridescence is structural. In the case of hummingbirds' iridescence, the top third of certain feathers have filmlike plate-lets with air bubbles that produce color by the process of interference. This is the same process that produces colors on soap bubbles.

© C.H. Greenewalt/VIREO

Above: This Red-tailed Comet is a good example of why hummingbirds have inspired people to poetry in order to describe them. The exquisite colors, the glittering iri-descence, the tail that's as long as the bird itself—all that in the smallest species of birds known. Other hummingbirds may have crests, ear tufts, and leg puffs as well, all in the tiniest package possible.

Hummingbirds have the fewest feathers of any bird, often less than one thousand, but they have the most densely distributed plumage. They have more feathers per square inch than any other bird. The density of their feathers helps them maintain their high body temperature in spite of the fact that they have no down feathers.

While iridescence is the most striking feature of hummingbirds, many of the Central and South American species have startlingly magnificent crests and tails as well. The Black-breasted Plovercrest (Stephanoxis lalandi) has an emerald-green crest that makes it look as if its head is in the shape of an exaggerated cone. The Horned Sungem (Heliactin cornuta) has a double crest of green, yellow, and red rising up out of its purple forehead. Other hummingbirds notable for their crests are the Adorable Coquette (Lophornis adorabilis), the Bearded Helmetcrest (Oxypogon guerinii), and the Rainbow-bearded Thornbill (Chalcostigma herrana).

The Doctor Bird, or Streamertail, of Jamaica has a tail 6 or 7 inches (15 or 17.5 cm) long, much longer, in fact, than the bird itself. The Booted Racket-tail (Ocreatus underwoodii) has two long bare tail feathers with rounded discs at the ends; the Crimson Topaz (Topaza pella) has two long tail feathers that cross in back; the Wire-crested Thorntail (Lophornis [Popelairia] popelairii) has a brilliant green crest that narrows to a few feathers that are as thin as wire, and a curious tail of three pairs of sharply pointed steel blue feathers with white shafts that are long on the outside and shorten progressively toward the middle.

A number of hummingbirds have such unusual tails that they have been named for them: Peruvian Sheartail (Thaumastura cora), Fork-tailed Emerald (Chlorostilbon canivetti), Ecuadorean Piedtail (Phlogophilus hemileucurus), Scissor-tailed Hummingbird (Hylonympha macrocerca), White-tailed Starfrontlet (Coeligena phalerata), Red-tailed Comet (Sappho sparganura), Fire-throated Metaltail (Metallura eupogon), Violet-tailed Sylph (Aglaiocercus coelestis), Slender-tailed Woodstar (Microstilbon burmeisteri), Sparkling-tailed Hummingbird (Tilmatura dupontii), Racket-tailed Coquette (Discosura longicauda), Marvelous Spatuletail (Loddigesia mirabilis), Black-bellied Thorntail (Popelairia langdorfii), and Green-tailed Trainbearer (Lesbia nuna). These are by no means all of the hummingbirds with strange and wonderful tails.

Certainly, the most spectacular element of hummingbird anatomy is its iridescent feathers. Not all hummingbirds are spectacularly feathered; those that live in dense, dark tropical rain forests where there is little sun to make their plumage glitter are quite dull in color. A South American group, hermits, are deprived of the usual bejeweled splendor; they are mostly brown, which renders them virtually invisible when perched. But those species that are iridescent have inspired people to poetry to adequately describe their brilliance.

© Wendy Shattil/Bob Rozinski

The underpart of the hummingbird usually has the least colorful and iridescent feathers, as this Copper-rumped Hummingbird shows.

Iridescence is a little magical, and it is not inaccurate to say that it's done with mirrors. I discovered this the first time I held an Anna's Hummingbird in my hand. I had hung two large baskets of fuchsias outside a pair of French windows that I kept open on summer days. The hummingbirds came often to feed, and one day one of them flew into the house. It flew around bumping into windows until I could get a soft dish towel over it. I was startled to find in my hand, not the brilliant red and green creature that had flown in, but a tiny, dowdy, drab little bird with black eyes. As I took it to the window to let it go, the sunlight struck its head at just the right angle and suddenly the lusterless, frightened creature was transformed into a living jewel again.

There are several ways that light can become iridescent. Structural colors, like a red sunset in a blue sky, are caused by microscopic particles like dust that scatter light into different wavelengths. Refracted colors occur when white light is broken into a colored spectrum, like the colors thrown off by a prism. Light that is both refracted and reflected, like sunlight through raindrops, causes rainbows. Interference is what makes colors appear on soap bubbles or in oil slicks on water.

With hummingbirds, the mirrors with which the magic is done are thin, transparent, filmlike platelets arranged like an intricate mosaic on the tips (the top one-third) of their feathers. The platelets contain air bubbles, and it is the thickness of the platelets and the amount of air inside them that determines exactly what part of the spectrum and thus which color is seen. The feathers on the bird's head (crown) and throat (gorget) have barbules that are like flat mirrors: The light that hits them can only be reflected in one direction. Therefore, the bird must be at the correct angle to the sun to create the iridescence, and the viewer must be at precisely the right angle to the bird to see its iridescence as well. All three—sun, observer, and hummingbird need to be lined up—the sun behind the observer and the hummingbird facing the sun for the magical colors to flash. From a different angle the color may change; without sunlight the bird may appear utterly drab. The feathers on the back are shaped differently, like concave mirrors. Light reflected off them bounces in all directions, so any time there is any light to reflect, it always appears as the same color.

Iridescent feathers are not as strong as those that are not, so the feathers essential to flight and maneuverability—the primary and secondary feathers of the wings and sometimes, tail feathers too—are not iridescent.

What is the purpose of the magnificent loveliness of these exquisite creatures? As far as science can determine, it has no purpose on earth except to dazzle the beholder. Males carefully orient themselves to the sun to show off their colors to best advantage when they do their spectacular aerial courtship displays for the females, but since the female seeks out the male by invading his feeding territory when she is ready to breed, color and iridescence don't seem to have much to do with the perpetuation of the species. Since the courtship display and the threat display to drive off intruders are in many hummingbird species distinctly similar, one half wonders if sex isn't a bit of an afterthought as far as the males are concerned. His role is to chase her off his territory, hers is to make sure he chases her into hers. After the moment of mating, the male goes back home to scare off any other intruders.

If the bright colors are intended to be threatening, it seems that the wicked little bill, the aerial agility, and the utter fearlessness that also characterize the hummingbird would serve that purpose sufficiently well. But what a lovely world to live in in which beauty need serve no purpose but to delight the eye.

Top: Feathers on the backs of hummingbirds are also iridescent, but the platelets on these feathers are shaped differently. Instead of being flat, as they are on the gorget, these platelets are like concave mirrors. No matter what angle the light comes from, they always reflect the same color. In the case of most hummingbirds, that color is green.

Bottom: The Horned Sungem is one of the most spectacular hummingbirds. The head alone has five colors, and the body has three more. The subject of this portrait objected to having his photograph taken: The fanned tail is a threat display.

FLIGHT: THEY SING WITH THEIR HANDS

Top Guns

Igor Sikorsky, who invented the helicopter, said he got his best design ideas for his invention from watching hummingbirds fly. Like hummingbirds, helicopters can lift off vertically, hover, fly forward, backward, and sideways. Helicopters, however, cannot fly upside-down; hummingbirds can.

If the daring "top gun" pilots of popular myth really wanted to be the best flyers in the world, they wouldn't bother aspiring to fly like an eagle; they'd pray to fly like a hummingbird. When it comes to flying, hummingbirds have no peer; in fact, no other bird even comes close. Hummingbirds can fly forward, backward, from side to side, and even upside-down; they can hover like a helicopter; and when they're showing off in courtship and threat displays, they can achieve dive speeds of 60 miles (96 km) per hour. The only thing a hummingbird can't do is soar; soaring requires broader wings than any hummingbird has.

Left: Hummingbirds are unique in that they fly by rotating the entire wing, with little or no flexing of the joints analogous to the human wrist and elbow. This is what makes it possible for them to hover and fly backward, which no other bird can do. (Some birds, like kestrels, can hover briefly by riding wind thermals, but they cannot sustain it without the lift from the thermal.)

Hummingbirds are not the fastest birds on earth; that honor goes to the duck hawk, which has been timed at between 160 and 180 miles (256 and 288 km) per hour. Swifts, believed to be hummingbirds' closest relatives, can fly as fast as 100 miles (160 km) per hour. There are reports in hummingbird literature where some species have been clocked at speeds up to nearly 60 miles (96 km) an hour, but tail winds may have had an influence in those tests. In wind-tunnel tests, Ruby-throated Hummingbirds top out at about 30 miles (48 km) an hour. These experiments were carried out by Crawford H. Greenewalt, an American ornithologist, whose children impudently dubbed the wind tunnel "Daddy's Torture Chamber" despite his protests that the birds came to no harm.

Pages 56–57: Hummingbirds are sexually dimorphic, the scientific way of saying that the males and females don't look alike. Males tend to be brilliantly colored, like this male Broad-tailed Hummingbird, while females tend to be well camouflaged, like this female Broad-tail (inset). Among the green leaves of a tree, the female is virtually invisible. Since she builds the nest and rears the babies alone—males have no role in perpetuating the species beyond fertilization—it is crucial to the survival of the species that she be inconspicuous to predators.

Walter Scheithauer timed two captive Blue-throated Sylphs *(Aglaiocercus kingi)* at speeds over 47 miles (75 km) per hour, but determined their average speed to be a more moderate 38.4 miles (61 km) per hour. Hummingbirds, the smallest of all birds, are still faster than most other birds. Most songbirds fly somewhere between 20 and 35 miles (32 and 56 km) per hour. To bring the comparison a bit closer to home, if human beings capable of running a four-minute mile, about top speed for humans, kept it up for an hour (which they couldn't), they would be running 15 miles (24 km) an hour, which gives one a tad more respect for hummingbirds.

Hummingbirds' flight muscles are anchored to an unusually large breastbone (sternum). The flight muscles constitute 25 to 30 percent of their total body weight, as much as 50 percent more than some other birds. This hummingbird is a Crowned Woodnymph, a South American species found from Mexico to Ecuador and in Argentina.

*H*ummingbirds *F*ly *W*ith *T*heir *H*ands

Hummingbirds can perform their extraordinary aerial acrobatics because their wings are unlike those of any other bird. Think of the bones of a bird's wing as being analogous to the bones of the human arm and hand. Most birds have wings that move (articulate) at the shoulder, elbow, and wrist. The leading edge of the wing, from shoulder to thumb, is a straight line. With each beat, the wing bends at the elbow and wrist. The easiest way to understand this folded wing structure is to pay close attention to skeletal anatomy the next time you order Buffalo wings, or roast chicken; the bones of the upper arm, forearm, and hand are quite easy to identify.

Hummingbird wings are entirely different. The upper arm and forearm bones are very short, and the elbow and wrist joints can't move. The upper arm and forearm form a V, a permanently bent elbow, attached to the shoulder at one end and the hand at the other. The shoulder joint to which the wing attaches can not only move in all directions, but can rotate about 180 degrees as well; this is why the hummingbird is such an aerial acrobat.

Hummingbird wings, anatomically and analogically speaking, are more hand than arm. Hummingbirds don't fly by flapping their arms as other birds do; hummingbirds fly with their hands. The flight feathers are attached to the three phalanges, which are analogous to human fingers. The flight feathers consist of ten primary and six or seven secondary feathers. (To imitate the stroke, pull your elbows up close to your body and move your hands in a figure-eight motion. That's how hummingbirds hover.) To fly forward, the hummingbird's wings describe a vertical oval parallel with its body. For the bird to fly backward, the wings describe a horizontal oval perpendicular to its head.

Double-Powered Flight

To accomplish these feats of flight, hummingbirds power their wings on both the down-stroke and the upstroke (recovery stroke). No other bird does this. All other birds power their wings only on the downstroke. This difference is readily apparent from the sheer mass of hummingbirds' pectoral muscles, which power their flight. These muscles represent 25 to 30 percent of hummingbirds' total body weight, and only 15 to 25 percent of the weight of other birds that are accomplished flyers. By comparison, the pectoral muscles in people constitute a mere 5 percent of their body weight. If a 150-pound (67.5-kg) person's pectorals were 25 to 30 percent of their body weight, they would have chest muscles weighing 38 to 45 pounds (17–20 kg) — that's one-quarter to nearly one-third of their weight. Not even the most ardent bodybuilder dreams of that! Like swifts and falcons, birds also built to fly fast, hummingbirds have exceptionally large breastbones (sternums), a deep keel to which the heavy-duty flight muscles are anchored.

Hummingbirds are the only birds that power their wings on both the upstroke and the downstroke. Other birds only power their wings on the downstroke. This hummingbird is a Black-breasted Plovercrest, a South American species found from Brazil to Argentina.

Below: The South American hermit hummingbirds, like this Band-tailed Barbthroat, eat far more insects than do the hummingbirds found in North America. While North American hummingbirds catch their prey on the wing, chasing them down by following every twist and turn the insect makes, the hermits are more likely to have bills adapted to extracting insects and nectar from tropical flowers.

For most birds, the upstroke is primarily intended to return the wing to position for another downstroke. The elevator muscles that bring the wing back up weigh only 5 to 10 percent of those that power the downstroke. In hummingbirds, the downstroke and upstroke muscles are powered just about equally; the upstroke (elevator) muscles weight 50 percent of the downstroke (depressor) muscles. That means hummingbirds proportionally have five to ten times more upstroke muscles than other birds.

Opposite page: Individual hummingbirds beat their wings at the same rate whether flying forward, backward, or hovering. The smaller hummingbird species have the fastest wing beat of any bird: eight wing beats per second in forward flight, and up to two hundred wing beats per second in the nosedives of courtship and territorial displays.

To reduce the stress on the flight muscles—in fact, to make it possible for the bird to lift itself into flight—the wing and leg bones of the hummingbird are hollow. The rest of the bones are not as solid as human bones, but porous. The porous bones are both lighter and stronger than solid bones because they are reinforced structurally by a series of internal struts. Because the bones are flexible and filled with air, they absorb and cushion impact better than solid bone, and can bend under blows that would break or shatter solid bone.

Wing Beats

Small hummingbirds—those with a wingspan of 1 to 2 inches (2.5–5 cm)—beat their wings thirty-eight to seventy-eight times per second. Large hummingbirds—those with a wingspan of $2^{1}/_{2}$ to $3^{1}/_{2}$ inches (6.25–8.75 cm)—beat their wings eighteen to twenty-eight times per second. In general, birds with small wings beat them faster than birds with longer or broader wings. Vultures, for example, those masters of soaring and cruising flight, flap their wings once every second.

Wingspan of birds is always measured from the wingtip to the first articulated joint. For all birds except hummingbirds, this is from tip to shoulder; for hummingbirds, it is from tip to wrist. This South American hummingbird is a Long-tailed Woodnymph, found along the coast of Brazil.

Wingspan, by the way, is always measured from wingtip to the first articulated joint. For hummingbirds this is from tip to shoulder, for all other birds it is from tip to wrist. Unlike most birds, hummingbirds cannot fold their wings neatly out of the way when they are perched or on the nest. The wings are so long in proportion to the body that they extend all the way to the tip of the tail.

Early investigators of hummingbird flight tried to determine the number of wing beats per second by sound. They tuned a violin string to the precise sound of a hovering hummingbird, then counted the number of vibrations of the string, which came to an astonishing—and inaccurate—two hundred beats per second. Later experimenters discovered the error when they realized that the sound audible to human ears was an overtone. The fundamental tone was too low for human hearing to detect, which meant it had a much lower rate of vibration.

When "Papa Flash," the venerable Professor Harold E. Edgerton of Massachusetts Institute of Technology, invented the strobe light, Crawford H. Greenewalt seized on the new technology as a way to secure photographic images of hummingbirds in flight. The hope was that the high-speed flash equipment would be fast enough to actually stop the wing on film, which would create a clear image of the hummingbird in flight, and provide a means of measuring how fast the wings beat. Motion pictures made with a camera attached to a stroboscope with a flash set at 1/100,000 second finally solved the wing-beat mystery. Greenewalt's film of a female Ruby-throated Hummingbird showed an average wing beat of fifty-two times per second, a far cry from the two hundred beats indicated by the violin string. Still, by odd coincidence there are some instances when the smaller hummingbirds achieve two hundred wing beats per second: Both the Ruby-throat and Rufous do it during their nuptial dives when they plummet toward earth at 80 miles (128 km) per hour.

Greenewalt also described hummingbirds as having "a constant speed motor." Each individual bird beats its wings at the same rate, varying no more than plus or minus 5 percent, whether hovering, flying forward or backward, making a fast getaway, or flying at top speed.

Hummingbirds Do Perch; They Don't Walk

Hummingbirds would rather fly than walk or hop even a few inches. Their feet appear to have no function beyond perching and scratching themselves. In 1931 the official Check-list for North American birds published by the American Ornithologists' Union (AOU) listed hummingbirds in the order *Micropodiformes*, meaning "small-footed." Curiously, the name was changed in the 1957 AOU Check-list to *Apodiformes*, which makes no sense at all since it means "footless," and hummingbirds are most assuredly not without feet. They have, in fact, four tiny toes, three in front and one in back, and tiny toenails to match. Perhaps the AOU is anticipating an evolutionary change in the near future: Evolutionists keep insisting that a key evolutionary principle is "use it or lose it," and since hummingbirds so rarely use their feet for walking, perhaps the compilers of the AOU Check-list are predicting that their tiny feet will eventually disappear entirely.

High-speed photographs have revealed that a hummingbird is actually in full flight before it ever lets go of the perch. Some birds use height and gravity to get themselves airborne. Auks and albatross drop off high cliffs into free fall, beating their wings until safely airborne, rather as one rolls a car downhill to pop the clutch for a compression start. Other birds, such as chickadees, push off the branch with their legs for a little extra lift to launch themselves. Large land birds run along the ground, flapping madly, until they become airborne. Not hummingbirds. There is no gradual revving up. It takes three wing beats, or 7/1,000 second for a hummingbird to achieve sufficient speed to lift off the branch. By the time the hummingbird is airborne, it's at almost full flight speed.

Hummingbirds also use their wings to keep their balance when they are perched, as people walking a balance beam will stretch out their arms and move them up and down until they achieve equilibrium. Anna's and Allen's Hummingbirds perched at a feeder tilt their heads up and their bodies back so far that to keep from falling over backward, they beat their wings to keep their balance, all the while clinging firmly to the perch.

Thomas Nuttall (1786–1859), the British-American naturalist, first saw a Rufous Hummingbird, shown here, on an expedition (1834–1836), and wrote John Audubon that: "…it seemed like a breathing gem, or magic carbuncle of glowing fire, stretching out its gorgeous ruff, as if to emulate the sun itself in splendour."

Hovering and Landing

It is often said that hummingbirds hover motionless while feeding. My observation is that they more often fly forward for a quick lick, then backward while their tongues flick in and out like a snake's, and fast forward again for another swift lick. Sometimes they perch quietly; sometimes they lean backward, wings beating in a blur, to keep their balance. I have rarely seen them hover motionless. Perhaps more amazing is that hummingbirds can approach a perch at dazzling speed, yet stop abruptly and land so lightly that even a feeder suspended from a long chain scarcely sways. This is an instance where the physical laws of mass and momentum connect with observable reality to create a minor miracle one can watch at any hummingbird feeder a dozen times a day. To understand the difference between your mass and the hummingbird's, imagine the impact and the sway you would create if you ran full speed into one of those bags football players practice tackling on. Now imagine hanging on with your toes.

Hummingbirds land as precisely as they take off. Just as the wings are in motion before the bird lets go of the perch, they are still in motion as it touches down. The female lowers herself onto the nest without even using her feet, settling as gently as a bit of down onto her eggs or nestlings. The positioning is so precise that she can land without even touching the edges of the nest, sinking gently into the center.

Opposite page: Hummingbirds land flaps down, just as airplanes do. This landing Broad-billed Hummingbird has its wings out and slanted down, and its tail spread to reduce its speed.

Below: Unlike other birds, a hummingbird's wings are still in motion when it touches down. Hummingbirds' landings are as gentle as thistledown; the female lowers herself into the nest without even using her feet. This Frilled Coquette is a South American hummingbird native to eastern and central Brazil.

Flying Backward and Upside-Down

Flying backward was one of the earliest phenomena of hummingbird flight the first European observers reported. Naturally, nobody believed them. Insects might fly backward, but birds? Never! The reporters even modified their descriptions to suggest that the hummingbird was, in fact, an insect that metamorphosed into a bird, and several claimed to have personally observed the metamorphosis. George Campbell, Duke of Argylle, a noted authority on English jurisprudence, dismissed the reports of birds that flew backward with the airy assurance that it was merely an optical illusion: Hummingbirds "fell backward" from the flowers on which they fed. The fact that he had never seen one, feeding or otherwise, in no way diminished his certainty on the subject.

Hummingbirds do, in fact, fly backward simply by slanting the angle of their wings, thanks to the extraordinary 180-degree mobility of the shoulder joint that distinguishes their wing structure from other birds. They reach back with their wings and scoop air forward, similar to the motion of swimming the backstroke.

Hummingbirds can also fly upside-down. Since both the downstroke and the upstroke are equally powered, the lift is nearly the same whether the bird is rightside-up or upside-down. Hummingbirds don't spend a lot of time flying upside-down. Most of the time, flying upside-down is used to make a quick getaway when the bird is startled; it spreads its tail and does a fast backward somersault, flies upside-down briefly, does a half roll and continues merrily on its way. Hummingbirds also fly sideways, but again, usually as an evasive maneuver.

If other birds are the conventional aircraft of the avian world, hummingbirds are the helicopters. While their wings actually resemble a movement closer to rowing than to the circular whirl of a rotor, the effect is very much the same. When helicopters hover, the rotor is on a plane parallel to the ground; and when it moves forward or backward, the rotor tilts in the appropriate direction, as do hummingbirds' wings. Helicopters can rise vertically without flying along a runway first, and hummingbirds can, too.

Hawking

Because of their aerial agility, hummingbirds can catch insects on the wing. They do not catch them by shooting out a sticky tongue as frogs do; their tongues are not sticky. Hummingbirds snap up flies as swallows do, with wide-open bills. They hover behind and below their prey, then snatch it out of the air by darting forward and upward. The bill functions like the angler's landing net: All the hummingbird has to do once the tidbit is caught is swallow. If the bird misses, it will dive instantly in an attempt to catch the insect, but if the insect falls to the ground, the bird ignores it entirely. If the bird misses and the insect keeps flying, the bird will follow every twist and turn of the prey in a

The joint at which the wing attaches to the body of the hummingbird has 180-degree mobility. It is this mobility that allows hummingbirds to fly backward, a motion similar to swimming the backstroke. Shown here is a South American hummingbird, the Black-bellied Thorntail, found in Peru and from Venezuela to Brazil.

breathtaking display of the mastery of flight, until the prey is caught. Hummingbirds prefer to take their prey on the wing, even to the point of startling sitting insects into taking flight so they can chase them down.

Fearlessness in Flight

The amazing maneuverability of hummingbirds makes them fearless in flight. Few other birds can fly fast enough to catch them; no other bird can match them for agility. And they do not hesitate to take on singlehandedly even the most fearsome birds of prey. Scott Weidensaul, an American naturalist, reports that hawks sharing the eastern migratory routes with the Ruby-throated Hummingbird are routinely harassed by their Lilliputian fellow travelers.

I once saw a dozen or more hummingbirds chasing a crow that was squawking and flapping madly over the roof of my house, and later found one of the crow's feathers on the ground. While most of the literature reports that hummingbirds do not cooperate socially (they do not flock together, nest together, or preen each other), they were clearly cooperating in driving off the crow.

No other bird can match the aerial agility and the astonishing acrobatics of the hummingbird. Its agility and speed gives it every right to be fearless. What predator could catch it on the wing? This Sparkling Violet-ear is a South American species found from Venezuela to Argentina.

Observers have long remarked on the cockiness and belligerence of hummingbirds defending their territory from other hummingbirds as well as birds of different species; it is true that females defend their nests fearlessly and effectively. Hummingbird mothers do not hesitate to drive off hawks, crows, scrub jays, chipmunks, snakes, and even yellow jackets (carnivorous wasps). Yet Robert Tyrrell reports that when he was photographing a nesting Anna's Hummingbird, she carefully inspected him, the ladder, sandbags, tripod, camera, and lights, and when she completed the investigation to her satisfaction, went busily on about her business. Photographers may represent a novelty in the lives of hummingbirds, but apparently not a threat.

Right: By watching a male Anna's Hummingbird for two days at the botanical gardens at the University of California at Berkeley, researcher Oliver Pearson determined that it would take the nectar of 1,022 fuchsia blossoms to satisfy the hunger (and caloric needs) of an Anna's Hummingbird for a single day.

Opposite page: With the rapid loss of rain forests in Central and South America, migratory hummingbirds are expanding their ranges farther and farther north. Hummingbird authority Dr. Alexander Skutch says in The Life of the Hummingbird, *"Let someone plant a flower garden almost anywhere from Canada to Argentina and Chile, in the lowlands of the mountains, amid humid forests or in irrigated deserts, and before long the bright blossoms will be visited by a tiny, glittering creature that hovers before them with wings vibrated into twin halos while it sucks their sweet nectar." Feeders and flowers make it possible for hummingbirds to extend their ranges since food supply is the most important factor in their survival.*

Pugnacious or Playful?

With feeding territories, I have seen more joyful exuberance than pugnacity. Certainly one hummingbird will drive another off a feeder, both streaking off in a high-speed, high-spirited chase. Moments later, one will return to feed, none the worse for wear. I also have seen one feed and then perch a few feet away, waiting in ambush for the next hummingbird to come along so it can dive-bomb it, and set off on another game of aerial tag. The birds remind me of children playing, hiding behind doors to jump out and startle one another, only to collapse in laughter, or teasing and jostling each other at a dinner table in those moments before an adult orders them to settle down. Never have I seen one harm another. None that I've observed have starved from being chased off momentarily. I have seen several perch quietly within a few inches of each other, and even share perches with each other, as mannerly and polite as you please, in spite of the fact that the vast majority of the literature suggests that hummingbirds are not gregarious.

© C.H. Greenewalt/VIREO

Although the vast majority of the literature suggests that hummingbirds are not gregarious, the birds have been observed sharing perches.

Perhaps the belligerence attributed to hummingbirds says more about the state of mind of the observers than irrefutable reality. Dr. Alexander Skutch, who lives in Costa Rica, states, "In the tropics, where resident birds are, on the whole, milder tempered than the migratory species of higher latitudes, I have rarely seen such stubborn conflicts as others have described in the North; here, the intruder is usually chased away without physical contact." My observations over the years have been the same, and they make me inclined to believe hummingbirds are more playful than pugnacious.

In aviaries, hummingbirds do much better with company than alone. Walter Scheithauer says:

> There is no billing and cooing as we have come to expect from other caged birds, like budgerigars (parakeets) and exotic finches. Each one keeps strictly to itself. And yet they need one another. Their aerial combats are an indispensable part of their life. Alongside bitterly contested fights, one can also observe mock battles that are evidently fought for the sheer joy of flight, the fun of performing skillful maneuvers, and from the sheer enjoyment of life. A hummingbird kept in a solitary state is a miserable shadow of what it could be if it had three or four companions of its own species in the cage. It is really only alive when it can indulge in squabbles.

Hummingbirds are quite curious about humans. I once sat beneath one of the feeders reading a newspaper while Allen's and Anna's Hummingbirds perched or hovered not 4 inches (10 cm) from my head, squeaking the whole while so I'd be sure to know that they were there. Charles James, an avid American hummingbird watcher, reports Anna's Hummingbirds literally eating out of his hand: They came to a freshly filled feeder he was holding in preparation to rehang it, when each bird hovered briefly to give him a quick once-over before perching or hovering, one at a time, at the feeder to eat. Alexander Skutch, a leading authority on tropical hummingbirds, speaks frequently of being approached within a few inches of his face by a Band-tailed Barbthroat *(Threnetes ruckeri)* bent on satisfying its curiosity, while the breeze from its wings fanned his face, which was hot and damp from his tramping through the dense vegetation of tropical lowlands. Walter Scheithauer related the story of a Brown Inca *(Coeligena wilsoni)* in his aviary that tried to tug out a few strands of his hair to build her nest. Many people have had the experience of a hummingbird hovering a few inches away to investigate red lipstick, a bright hat, or scarf.

Hummingbirds have good memories. They remember not only the location of flowers and feeders, but recognize individuals as well. One of the pioneer studies of hummingbird feeding habits was done by Althea Sherman of Iowa in 1907. The hummingbirds associated her with her feeders, and when the feeders were empty, would hover around her until she filled them. The Ruby-throats remembered her even after a year and a 4,000-mile (6,400-km) migration. Lisa Salmon has fed the hummingbirds at 4:00 P.M. at her home outside Montego Bay in Jamaica for more than thirty years, and they all come on time.

Above: Hermit hummingbirds like this Band-tailed Barbthroat are most often found in the equatorial lowland forests of the Amazon basin. As a group, hermits are the plainest of all the hummingbirds; iridescence doesn't show where there is little sun to make the feathers gleam and glitter. Band-tailed Barbthroats distinguish themselves by singing elaborate songs of deep melancholy at the start of the rainy season.

Left: Since several hummingbird species are expanding their ranges, year-round feeders may well mean the difference between survival and death for these pioneers. (Hummingbirds have been known to visit feeders even in driving snowstorms.) The formula for nectar is one part sugar to four parts water; it need not be colored red with food coloring, as hummingbirds come for the sweetness, not the color. Hummingbirds prefer sucrose (plain white granulated sugar) to glucose, and glucose to fructose.

Hummingbirds Sing With Their Hands

Hummingbirds sing with their hands, so to speak, for it is the humming of their wings that gave them their name. For most hummingbirds, the humming is simply the sound of the air movement from their rapidly beating wings, but for a few species, the wings are specially designed to create sound. When doing nose dives in courtship or threat displays, hummingbirds increase the speed of their dives by beating their wings until the usual humming becomes a sharp hiss. The wings of the Broad-tailed Hummingbird *(Selasphorus platycercus)* are notched at the tips, producing a metallic trill in normal flight and a sharp whistle when diving. The Lucifer Hummingbird *(Calothorax lucifer)* has been described as buzzing like a hornet. In courtship, the male Little Hermit *(Phaethornis longuemareus)* manages to make his wings buzz more loudly than in ordinary flight. The male Anna's puts the final touch on his courtship and threat displays by plunging downward in a power dive that ends inches over the head of the female or enemy, flying straight into the sun to illuminate his iridescent gorget in a blaze of glory, then finishes the performance with an explosive noise made with his tail. Beyond attributing the special sounds of courtship displays to attenuated or otherwise modified wing or tail feathers, no one knows quite how the hummingbirds create these sounds.

Flight displays for territorial defense are, for the most part, indistinguishable from courtship displays for the North American hummingbird species. South American hummingbirds found in rain forests, where flight displays might go unnoticed amid the dark, dense foliage, form singing assemblies instead. The males sing in groups to attract the females, a sort of hummingbird glee club. The hummingbird below is a Black-thighed Puffleg, found in Colombia and Ecuador.

© William B. Folsom

© D. Wechsler/VIREO

A SERENADE OF SQUEAKS

Unlike their northern cousins, the hummingbirds of Central and South America live in rain forests where the dense vegetation limits aerial displays; the males attract females by singing rather than by flying. Hummingbirds' voices don't carry far, so they form an all-male chorus called a singing assembly. Long-tailed Hermits *(Phaethornis superciliosus)* may gather in groups of more than one hundred males. As a group, the Hermits have the dullest plumage of all hummingbirds. Living in heavy jungles where sunlight rarely penetrates makes iridescent plumage irrelevant, as there is little light to make it flash and glitter. Instead, each male perches about 3 feet (.9 m) off the ground where he is so perfectly camouflaged by matching dead brown leaves that he would be invisible if he did not wag his white-tipped tail constantly, like a musician keeping time with his foot.

More brilliantly colored hummingbirds, such as the Blue-throated Goldentail *(Hylocharis eliciae)*, Green Violet-ear *(Colibri thalassinus)*, and Violet-headed Hummingbirds *(Klais guimeti)*, eliminate the problem of little sunlight by performing at the very tops of trees, where their feathers can flash to advantage. And there they sing, each on its own personal perch, day after day. The White-eared Hummingbird often selects two perches, one high and one low, between which he alternates. The singing males are always within hearing of each other, and often within sight.

Anna's Hummingbirds are the only North American species known to sing. The song is more complex than the songs of many songbirds, despite the fact that Anna's lack the part of the brain that neurophysiologists have identified as being the most important in learning songs.

73

This Colorful Puffleg clearly shows the powder-puff leg ornaments for which it was named. A South American species, the Colorful Puffleg is found nowhere on earth but in Colombia. There are 135 species of hummingbird found in Colombia; only Ecuador has more.

The songs heard in the singing assemblies are intriguing because all the males in any particular assembly sing songs that are virtually identical. Birds of the same species in another assembly only a short distance away may differ so completely that the inclination is to believe they are birds of a different species. (Most birds' songs are species-specific, and most birds can be identified on the basis of their song alone.) Since hummingbirds learn their songs from other males, it seems likely that young birds joining their first singing assembly learn the song sung there.

When and how much each hummingbird sings varies according to its species. Band-tailed Barbthroats in Costa Rica sing at the start of the rainy season; Violet-headed Hummingbirds and Blue-throated Goldentails celebrate the dry season in song; the Little Hermit sings lustily all year long, except when the rains are heaviest and the height of the dry season. Rufous-tailed Hummingbirds begin singing with the first light of dawn and stop soon after sunrise; Blue-chested Hummingbirds *(Amazilia [Polyerata] amabilis)* sing in the morning and again in the afternoon; Green Violet-ears and some Hermits sing so incessantly all day, stopping rarely to refresh themselves with nectar, that Skutch remarks that "they appear to be highly efficient machines for transmuting nectar into squeaks." The only North American species known to sing is the Anna's, and those at my house sing for twenty minutes or more without pause.

Most hummingbirds can't sing for beans, but some have songs that fall sweetly on the ear. The Little Hermit's song is reported to have a pleasant lilt and cadence, the Band-tailed Barbthroat has an elaborate song of deep melancholy, the Wine-throated Hummingbird has a gently varied song, and the Wedge-tailed Sabrewing *(Campylopterus curvipennis)* is referred to as the "nightingale hummingbird."

Believe it or not, hummingbirds hum. Closing their beaks, humping their backs, tilting up their bills, and swelling their throats, males pour forth a song *sotto voce*, precisely the way people hum to themselves. Adult males will take a break from their more audible song in singing assemblies to hum, and immature male Scaly-breasted Hummingbirds *(Phaeochroa cuvierii)* and Purple-throated Mountain-gems *(Lampornis calolaema)* hum when they are fed by their mothers.

Flight Endurance and Migration

The amount of time that hummingbirds spend in flight varies considerably. Walter Scheithauer watched a captive White-ear *(Hylocharis leucotis)* for sixteen hours; of those sixteen hours, it spent fifteen on the wing. On another occasion, when he was attempting to photograph a female Lucifer, it remained in flight for four solid hours while he stood, poised, alert, and ready to snap the photo the moment the bird hovered at the flower put up for its delectation. Just for the record, the photo was never shot; after four hours, Scheithauer gave up, utterly defeated, and exhausted just from waiting.

One of the major mysteries of hummingbird migration that puzzled scientists for years was posed by the Ruby-throated Hummingbird. The mystery was this: How could a bird as tiny as a hummingbird fly non-stop over nearly 500 miles (800 km) of open ocean as the Ruby-throated Hummingbird does on its 2,000 or more mile (3,200 km or more) migration from as far south as Panama to as far north as Nova Scotia? For many years scientists calculated that it was impossible: Hummingbirds

The Magnificent Hummingbird has been renamed over and over. First classified in 1827 by a British naturalist as Trochilus fulgens, *which means "shining humming-bird," it was also named by two French naturalists as* L'Eugenes de Rivoli. Eugenes *means "well-born," and the name was translated as "Rivoli's princeling," in honor of the Duke of Rivoli. In 1856 John Gould resolved the issue by taking one name from each and classifying the bird as* Eugenes fulgens, *which in English is "shining princeling"; the common name was Rivoli's Hummingbird. In 1983 the American Ornithological Union Check-list changed the common name to Magnificent Hummingbird; that same year Paul Johnsgard's* The Hummingbirds of North America *listed the Latin name as* Heliodoxa fulgens, *which translates as "shining glory of the sun." About the only fact on which everyone agreed was this species' beauty.*

© T.J. Ulrich/VIREO

When migrating, Ruby-throated Hummingbirds fly nonstop 500 miles (800 km) across the Gulf of Mexico. They average 25 miles (40 km) an hour, flying without a moment's rest for no less than twenty hours and for as long as twenty-six hours.

surely could not store sufficient fat to sustain the energy needed to make the journey. Ruby-throated Hummingbirds did not know their migration route across the Gulf of Mexico was considered impossible—they did it twice a year.

Later, scientists realized that their laboratory calculations of flight speed and caloric output were incorrect. What actually happens is that Ruby-throated Hummingbirds gorge themselves just before migrating, adding 40 to 50 percent more weight than normal, going to .11 to .16 ounce (3–4 g). (The equivalent of a 150-pound [67.5-kg] person preparing a walk of 500 miles [800 km] by putting on 60 to 75 pounds [27–34 kg], starting the trek weighing 210 to 225 pounds [94–101 kg], and not eating on the way.) The added weight slows the bird down, but the added fat allows it to fly longer. Robert Lasiewski, an authority on hummingbirds, estimates that by oxidizing .07 ounces (2 g) of fat a Ruby-throated could fly for twenty-six hours. At an average speed of 25 miles (40 km) an hour, that would carry it from Yucatán to Louisiana with a margin of safety of more than 150 miles (240 km), a reasonable allowance for headwinds or crosswinds that might blow it off course. At an average of 52 wing beats per second for Ruby-throated Hummingbirds, that adds up to 187,200 wing beats per hour, and 4,867,200 wing beats nonstop for twenty-six hours across the open ocean of the Gulf of Mexico. The other 1,500 miles (2,400 km) must be a cinch by comparison.

Perhaps the most amazing flight records belong to the tiny Rufous Hummingbird, which migrates over 5,000 miles (8,000 km) per year, 2,500 miles (4,000 km) each way from Alaska to Mexico. In the spring it leaves central Mexico (Zacatecas, Jalisco, the state of Mexico, and Michoacan) to fly across the Sea of Cortés (Gulf of California), along more than 1,000 miles (1,600 km) of California coast, over Oregon, Washington, British Columbia, to Alaska. The coastal mountains rise to elevations over 15,000 feet (4,500 m), forcing the hummingbirds to turn out over the open sea or climb to 8,000 feet (2,400 m) to take the passes through the mountains. The Rufous has been seen by sailors miles from land over the Gulf of Alaska, notorious for its inclement weather. In autumn, it flies south and east, traveling through the Rocky Mountains.

Equally amazing, hummingbirds migrate, not in flocks, but each one entirely alone. Typically, the males leave first, followed weeks later by the females, and on the southward-bound journey after breeding, the females are followed several weeks later by their young. No one knows how the young birds, flying alone on their first migration with no adults to guide them, find their way hundreds of miles, or in the case of the Rufous and Ruby-throat, thousands of miles, home to their southern wintering grounds. But they do.

The Rufous Hummingbird has the longest migration of any hummingbird, more than 5,000 miles (8,000 km) a year. It flies north from central Mexico to Alaska and the Yukon Territory and back again.

COURTSHIP, MATING, AND NESTING

Humans have only rarely been able to observe hummingbirds mating. Most of the copulations described are now believed to be descriptions of aggressive behavior. In some species, the female seeks out the male by invading his territory; in others, the females come to where males have a singing assembly. Among certain hermits, a species where the sexes look very much alike, all the female has to do to signal her mating intentions is remain still long enough for the male to mount her. Observations in aviaries suggest that males attain copulation primarily by intimidation, rather than courtship. The male mounts the female as she perches, sometimes holding on to the feathers of her neck with his beak, as in the photograph above.

© C.H. Greenewalt/VIREO

Courtship

Courtship among North American hummingbirds echoes the worst laments of single women everywhere. First off, he never calls. She has to go find him, and get his attention by invading his territory. His response is to perform his threat display, which doubles, in emergencies such as these, as a courtship display; mostly, it's showing off in the most blatant style. He carefully orients himself to the sun so that his iridescent plumage will blaze in the most dazzling manner. Then he takes off like a rocket, 75 to 150 feet (22–45 m) into the sky, flies nearly out of sight, pauses momentarily at the top, then drops like a bomb, bill down, to within 1 to 2 inches (2–5 cm) of her head. In the case of the male Anna's, he finishes the performance off by popping his tail to make a loud, high-pitched whistle. The female sits and watches politely. If she gets lucky, he'll follow her home. Mating takes three to five seconds, then he disappears. The female finishes her nest, lays the eggs, and tends the young alone. Male hummingbird behavior is every woman's worst nightmare.

© Wendy Shattil/Bob Rosinski

Each species of hummingbird has its own pattern of courtship or threat display. The Anna's, which was described above, may also sing for a moment at the highest point of the display, just before diving. Anna's, Allen's, and Costa's Hummingbirds usually fly along a narrow arc in the sky; the male Ruby-throated Hummingbird typically describes a wider arc. Anna's, Allen's, Costa's, Rufous, Calliope, Black-chinned, Broad-tailed, and Ruby-throated males all display alone, but there is one documented report of three male Broad-tailed Hummingbirds displaying together. The male Anna's usually repeats its display three to eight times in a row, although as few as one and as many as a dozen have been reported. The shrill whistle made by the Anna's tail feathers is loud enough to be heard hundreds of feet away.

The display of the Allen's male is quite different. He flies in shallow arcs 20 to 30 feet (6–9 m) above the head of the female. At each end of the arc, he spreads his tail and hangs, quivering, for a moment in the air. After several repetitions, he spirals slowly upward, bill pointed toward the sky. At the peak of his flight, he dives at top speed, his primary feathers sounding a high trill as he plunges toward earth. He may repeat this display several times.

Male Broad-tailed Hummingbirds, like the one below, are one of the few North American species that have been seen to perform a courtship display in a group. This has only been observed once, in Colorado in 1972 when D. P. Barash observed three males performing together.

Opposite page: Male hummingbirds do not participate in the perpetuation of the species beyond fertilizing the female. Males occupy themselves primarily with defending feeding territories. In some species, females signal their willingness to mate by invading the male's territory. He responds by chasing her out; this is sometimes followed by copulation.

Another display, which scientists suspect is more specifically a mating display than the extravagant and dramatic aerial swoops and dives, is called the shuttle display. It is not well known or often observed because it is typically performed in dense undergrowth. The male flies back and forth a few inches over the female's head several times; each swing covers about 10 inches (25 cm). The female watches these antics like a spectator at a tennis match. All of the most widely known North American species perform this short shuttle display (Anna's, Allen's, Costa's, Rufous, Calliope, Black-chinned, Broad-tailed, and Ruby-throated), but each species adds its own particular sound. Some vibrate their feathers; others, like the Anna's and Costa's, sing, or, more accurately, twitter and squeak. This performance is followed by a high-speed chase and, presumably, mating. As is so often the case, the male chases the female until she catches him.

Anna's Hummingbirds are the only North American species known to sing. (To be absolutely accurate, Costa's Hummingbirds do have a brief song, described by one highly respected ornithologist as "a screeching, buzzing, whining thing.") The Anna's songs are more complex than the songs of many songbirds, despite the fact that neurophysiologists have found that Anna's Hummingbirds begin singing with a juvenile song, the hummingbird equivalent of baby talk. The adult song is crystallized at three-and-a-half to four months. One Anna's song was transcribed as, "$B_1B_2B_2 - B_1B_2B_1 - S_1S_2S_2 - B_1B_2B_2$," which may be read as Buzz one, Buzz two, Buzz two; Buzz one, Buzz two, Buzz one; Squeak one, Squeak two, Squeak two; Buzz one, Buzz two, Buzz two. It does have a certain charm to it.

Many South American hummingbirds congregate in specific places where the males perform group courtship displays. These places are called leks or arenas, and remain the same from year to year. There may be no more than three or four males or as many as one hundred. The closest human comparison, perhaps, is the Latin custom of the promenade, where young men and women dress up in their most attractive clothes to walk in the evening around a central plaza, men in one direction, women in the other; they pretend to ignore each other, while actually conducting the most detailed inspection. Perhaps they got the idea from the hummingbirds.

Where male hummingbirds gather in leks, the females are attracted by the sound, and most often, the female chooses the male. The two birds may perform a nuptial ceremony at the male's display station and mate at once, or the full courtship ceremony and coition may be performed discreetly out of sight.

Some species, like the Little Hermit, perform flight displays. Alexander Skutch says that the male arches his head and tail until he resembles a "miniature boat with high-peaked prow and stern," and floats daintily over the head of the female, dipping toward her, wings buzzing loudly. The Rufous Hermit *(Phaethornis ruber)* sticks out his exceedingly long white tongue at the female while she sings to him. Other species perform the courtship flight together, flying side by side, etching on the sky more loops and whorls

Hummingbirds are polygamous; the males mate with several females, and the females mate with several males. There is no pairbonding among hummingbirds. These two hummingbirds are a male and a female Frilled Coquette, a South American species.

than a valentine written in a Victorian schoolmistress's fine Spencerian hand. They stop the aerial acrobatics long enough to hover bill-to-bill or wing-to-wing every now and again, but always vanish out of sight before mating. Wine-throated *(Atthis ellioti)* and Green Violet-ear Hummingbirds combine the two displays by singing in flight. Andean Hillstars trace high upside-down U's in the air and finish their display with a flourish of loops. The courtship continues in the female's nesting territory, where she feeds him repeatedly as though he were a fledgling. No other hummingbird does anything even vaguely similar. In fact, a female feeding a male is most unusual among birds in general since nearly all nuptial feeding is from male to female.

The only species in North America that perform in leks are the Blue-throated, *(Lampornis clemenciae)*, White-eared, and Berylline Hummingbirds. Coition is presumed, but dense foliage and swift flight being what they are, it has seldom been observed.

Hummingbirds are described as polygynous, which means that the males mate with more than one female, but in fact, the females also mate with more than one male, and so are polyandrous. Perhaps it would be more accurate to describe hummingbirds as polygamous.

Mating

Obviously, mating does take place. Hummingbirds do have babies. But coition has rarely been observed, and many of the instances that have been reported are suspect. Most experts are convinced that most reports of observed matings are, in fact, descriptions of aggressive behavior, not copulation. Some ornithologists believe that for some species of hummingbirds, courtship does not exist at all, but that the male simply overpowers the female into sex. The male mounts the female as she perches, sometimes holding onto the feathers of her neck with his beak. The egg formed in the female is fertilized by sperm deposited in the oviduct during copulation.

Pair relationship in other birds varies from mere mating (sandpipers) to pair bonding for the period of parenting (Bewick's wrens) to lifetime pairing (greylag geese and trumpeter swans). Among nearly all North American hummingbirds, pair bonding lasts as long as it takes to mate, which is to say, three to five seconds. Even though both a male and female hummingbird of the same species may be seen in the same territory at the same feeder, it is not accurate to refer to them as a "pair." For all practical purposes, North American hummingbirds don't pair.

In very rare cases, male hummingbirds have been reported sitting on eggs and feeding nestlings, but the reports are insufficiently documented; in none of these instances was the male's sex verified. The issue is further clouded by the fact that a variety of female hummingbirds occasionally sport plumage sufficiently similar to that of their male counterparts that their sex has been accurately determined only by dissection. However, there are a few reliable reports of male Anna's, Sword-billed, and Violet-eared Hummingbirds guarding nests.

Every hummingbird species has a different mating display. These Frilled Coquettes are touching bills, probably as part of their courtship.

Even in tropical areas, most hummingbirds have a specific breeding season. They lay eggs at a time when few other birds are nesting, at the beginning of the dry season. In the mountains of Central America, they breed from October to January. There are a few exceptions. The Andean Hillstar breeds all year in Ecuador, but not in Peru or Chile, and Anna's and Allen's Hummingbirds have been reported to breed year-round in southern California.

*N*esting

A female hummingbird begins her nest before mating: More than half of the nest is finished before she mates. Hummingbird nests are well hidden and well camouflaged. They are so beautifully ornamented that the correct scientific term is "decorated." The purpose of the decorations of lichens and feathers is to camouflage the nest from predators and prying eyes.

BUILDING THE NEST

The female begins the nest before she sets out to find a male willing to oblige her for three to five seconds. It is one-half to two-thirds finished before she mates. She may finish the nest while she is sitting on the eggs, and will continue to decorate it while she is caring for the nestlings.

In the collection of hummingbird nests at the California Academy of Sciences in San Francisco, there are nests that were built in live oaks, redwoods, bays, eucalypts, as well as one on a cholla cactus *(Opuntia)*, and another on a sword fern frond. Several nests were also found in blackberry brambles. Whether that was because people eat blackberries rather than redwoods, and so are more likely to find nests built there, or because the prickliness of the blackberry bramble provides additional protection for the nest is anybody's guess.

The nests in the collection were those of Ruby-throated, Anna's, Allen's, Calliope, Costa's, and Rufous Hummingbirds. Some nests were soft and smooth on the outside, others were heavily textured with lichens and bark fibers. They ranged in color from charcoal gray to the color of old ivory. Most had been collected in the 1880s and 1890s, and were labeled with tags identifying the species, where it was found, and who found it, all written with a fine Spencerian hand in black ink that had long since faded to sepia. Most were heavily ornamented, woven of mosses, leaves, bark fibers, comfortably lined with thistledown, and richly decorated (camouflaged) with lichens and feathers. All of the nests were 1 to 1½ inches (2–4 cm) from the branch to the rim, and 1½ to 2 inches (4–5 cm) in diameter. They are shallower inside from the thick lining. The nests are not rigid, but soft and pliable. Some looked to be made of tan cotton candy. They were bound to the branch and held together with cobwebs.

Each species has its own style of nest. Some are cup-shaped, some are cone-shaped, and some are slung over the branch like saddlebags. One of the most interesting nests is that of the Sooty-capped Hermit *(Phaethornis augusti)*. The nest hangs from a single strand of a spider's web from an overhead projection. The cable is attached to one side of the nest, which causes it to tilt precariously. The female counterbalances the tilt by fastening small lumps of dry clay or pebbles to the bottom of the nest with cobweb to keep it level. The Bronzy Hermit *(Glaucis aenea)* and Band-tailed Barbthroat build loose, open nests of thin, stiff rootlets and moss and liverwort stems. The nests dry rapidly, which is important where drenching rains are common, but they offer little insulation, although this is not a serious consideration in warm, tropical lowlands.

Female hummingbirds are extraordinary architects. Their nests blend so perfectly with their surroundings that a person can stand inches from the nest, stare directly at it, and not see it. I have been trying to find the nest of the Anna's Hummingbird that I am certain has lived in a hawthorn tree in my yard for five years.

Nesting materials include hair, fur, bits of insect sheds and cocoons, and dandelion down, which may be collected on the wing. At my old house I saved dryer lint all summer and autumn, then tucked handfuls of it in the trees in November when the Anna's Hummingbirds start building their nests. In our new house, I saw an Anna's female tug the fiber out of some exposed insulation. It's rated R-9, one of the highest ratings, so I'm sure her babies were warm.

Each species has its own nest-building style. This is the nest of a Black-chinned Hummingbird.

The females use their bills, breasts, and feet to build the nests, which take anywhere from a day to two weeks to make. They use their bills to tug loose and carry all their nesting materials, and to weave them into place, poking, prodding, and pulling them into proper shape. The bill is the needle that weaves the exterior of the nest. The female pushes the nest into its cupped shape by pressing her breast against it as she hovers. The rim angles inward slightly to form a seal with the mother's body so that no warmth escapes; the rim is also built higher to make the nest deeper after the eggs are laid. The female presses the lining into place with her feet. Esther Quesada Tyrrell, who provided the text for Robert Tyrrell's photographs in *Hummingbirds: Their Life and Behavior*, says the female accomplishes flattening the lining by "running or jogging on it." As little as hummingbirds like to walk, 2 inches (5 cm) seems like a fair distance for an expectant mother to jog.

The Broad-tailed, Rufous, and Calliope Hummingbirds that migrate into the Rocky Mountains of Colorado and Wyoming build nests so well insulated that the eggs under a brooding female maintain a night temperature of 95° to 97°F (33° to 36°C) even when the air temperature is only 46° to 47°F (7° to 8°C). The temperature of the eggs in an Anna's nest was measured at 50°F (28°C) higher than the air temperature.

LAYING AND CARING FOR THE EGGS

Hummingbirds lay the smallest eggs of any bird in the world. The eggs are less than $\frac{1}{2}$ inch (1.25 cm) long, weigh less than .02 ounce (5 g) and are elliptical in shape. The eggs typically weigh from 10 to 20 percent of the mother's total body weight. That's roughly equivalent to a 150-pound (67.5-kg) woman giving birth to a 15-to-30-pound (7–13-kg) baby. In the case of the Vervain Hummingbird, the eggs weigh 34 percent of the mother's weight. To go back to our 150-pound (67.5-kg) pregnant woman, that's the equivalent of delivering a 51-pound (23-kg) baby. To venture briefly into early childhood development, a good-sized baby weighs 7 pounds (3 kg), a large baby weighs 9 pounds (4 kg), and most children do not weigh 51 pounds (23 kg) until they are six or seven years old.

Hummingbirds usually lay two long, narrow eggs that resemble large jelly beans. Newly laid eggs are translucent when held up to the light, and the shells have a pale pinkish cast. They become more opaque with age. One early researcher thought the eggs looked so like candies, that he feared someone might eat his specimen thinking they were bon-bons. The largest eggs are those of the Giant Hummingbird — $\frac{3}{4}$ inch by $\frac{1}{2}$ inch (1.8 cm by 1 cm) — and the smallest are those of the Calliope Hummingbird at $\frac{1}{3}$ inch by $\frac{1}{2}$ inch (.93 cm by 1 cm).

Hummingbirds lay their eggs in the morning. Typically, the eggs are laid two days apart. The eggs need very high temperatures to incubate — around 90°F (32°C) — and all the heat comes from the mother's body. To generate the necessary heat, the

The nest of the Reddish Hermit is one of the most interesting of all hummingbird nests. Typically suspended from a leaf, such as a palm, Reddish Hermit nests are supported on their undersides along the leaf. They ordinarily have a long "trailer" of leaves or scraps of leaves hanging from the bottom, as this one does. The large leaves to which the nests are attached protect the nest from rain and most terrestrial predators.

© C.H. Greenewalt/VIREO

© Wendy Shattil/Bob Rosinski/Tom Stack & Associates

mother fluffs out her feathers to place the eggs against her brood patch, a section of her breast that has a high concentration of blood vessels which transmit her body heat through her skin to the eggs. Some species (or individuals) begin incubating as soon as the first egg is laid, others not until the second is laid.

Esther Quesada Tyrrell declares that the mother does not leave her eggs in cold weather or when it's raining, but that would be almost impossible for an Anna's Hummingbird, which nests in December as far north as British Columbia: she would starve. In the San Francisco Bay area it is often cold and/or rainy for days at a time in December and January, and this is even truer farther north. The Anna's is one of the earliest breeding birds, perhaps the earliest, in all of North America.

Black-chinned Hummingbirds prefer to nest near water, usually along streams at the bottom of a canyon, most often in deciduous trees such as willows, cottonwoods, alders, sycamores, and valley oaks. They are the most common nesting hummingbird in Texas, where they are usually found in agave-cactus desert and juniper-oak woods. Researcher Frank Bené theorizes that the nesting of Black-chinned Hummingbirds in and around Phoenix, Arizona, is due to the presence of irrigated gardens whose flowers provide the necessary nectar.

Above: During nesting the female Broad-tail leaves the nest to feed about fifteen minutes before sunrise, and makes her last feeding foray at sunset. She leaves the nest an average of ninety times a day, sixty times to feed and thirty times for short periods.

Pages 90–91: Broad-tailed Hummingbird nests are usually built on low, horizontal branches and are well camouflaged. Inset, top left: Typical nesting trees are spruce (shown here), pine, fir, aspen, alder, cotton-wood, and willow. The nests are decorated with lichens, shreds of bark, fine leaves, and other bits of plants. Broad-tailed Hummingbirds may return to the same nesting place year after year. Inset, below right: The time from when the Broad-tailed female lays the eggs until the young are fledged is approximately forty days. The Broad-tailed Hummingbird rarely raises more than one brood each season, though a few second broods have been reported. Two babies is the usual number, as in this photograph.

Hummingbirds typically set on their eggs from 60 to 80 percent of the day, leaving the eggs unattended as few as 10 and as often as 110 times a day. The mother usually sets longer in the afternoon than in the morning, sometimes as long as three hours at a time. Absences often last less than a minute and seldom longer than a half-hour. Since hummingbirds feed only during the day, the mother goes all night without food, which makes eating in the morning imperative. She leaves the eggs only to feed, to gather nesting materials (especially sticky and elastic cobweb, which Alexander Skutch calls "the indispensable cement of avian architects," to bind her nest more firmly together), and to defend the nest.

To make sure all sides of the egg are warmed equally, the mother turns the eggs with her bill as she hovers beside the nest. On the nest, she may use either her feet or her bill to rotate the eggs. In hot weather she raises her body off the eggs to cool them, or stands inside the nest, shading the eggs from the sun with her body. If she began incubating when the first egg was laid, it will hatch first; if she began incubation when the second egg was laid, the eggs will hatch at the same time. The incubation period is anywhere from fifteen to twenty-two days. The incubation period may be longer if temperatures are very low.

© Wendy Shattil/Bob Rosinski

The young are nourished in the egg by the nutrients in the yolk. They breathe through the shell, which is porous enough that oxygen passes in and carbon dioxide passes out. When the yolk is gone, the egg hatches. The newborn pecks its way out of the shell using the egg tooth, a temporary bony projection on the tip of its bill that disappears after hatching. The process of pecking its way out of the egg is called "pipping." After the newborns are hatched, the mother removes the broken bits of shell from the nest so their odor does not attract predators.

The inner lining of the hummingbird babies' mouths is bright yellow, and scientists hypothesize that the color stimulates the mother to feed the babies. Babies are born blind, featherless, and ugly as can be. It can take from eighteen days to twenty-six days for the babies to get all their feathers.

CARING FOR THE YOUNG

Once born, the baby hummingbird resembles nothing so much as an especially tiny, remarkably ugly, blind, black frog. It has no feathers, no down, no bill, and its huge eyes are sealed shut. It is completely helpless, and entirely dependent on its mother for warmth. Hummingbirds never develop down as most birds do; instead they develop pinfeathers within a few days of hatching, and by the time they are a week or two old, they have enough feathers to maintain their own body temperature. By the time a pair of Anna's nestlings could thermoregulate themselves (thirteen days), the temperature of the nest was measured at 86°F (48°C) higher than the air temperature.

Above: A mother hummingbird regurgitates food into her babies' crops by inserting her bill into their mouths and bringing up food from her own crop. The babies' crops become hugely swollen and stick out from their necks like a goiter.

Opposite page: The hummingbird nest is flexible: the sides expand to accommodate the babies as they grow. The mother may build the nest higher as the young grow, but still she's raising a family in a house not much bigger than an American quarter.

The young are hatched with crops, pouchlike enlargements of the esophagus in which food is stored or partially digested, that are enormous by comparison with the rest of their bodies. The mother feeds the young by inserting her bill into each baby's mouth and regurgitating food from her own crop. She feeds them in such quantities that within a few days the crop protrudes from the sides of their necks like an immense goiter. She feeds the babies from one to three times per hour.

Observers say that watching a mother hummingbird feed her babies is terrifying. It looks a lot like a sword-swallowing act with a blind sword-swallower. Walter Scheithauer never saw a Sword-billed Hummingbird, the longest-billed hummingbird, feed its young, but he once remarked that it must be an alarming act as the bird's bill is longer than the bird itself. As it was, he was amazed that nowhere in the literature is it recorded that some mother hummingbird perched or hovered too close and impaled her own nestling.

The nestlings begin begging for food before their eyes open. The sound of the mother's wings or the feeling of her moving in the nest makes them open their mouths for food. The insides of their mouths are bright yellow, which scientists believe stimulates the mother to feed them.

Hummingbird nests are remarkably clean. The mother cleans up after the hatchlings the first few days, tosses feces over the side of the nest, and carries them away or swallows them. Older nestlings shoot their feces over the edge of the nest. Even tiny nestlings make their way to the edge of the nest, practically standing on their heads to extend their posterior high enough, and excrete outside the nest.

By the time they are sixteen days old, the young birds are preening their feathers, sticking out their wings and tongues, and exploring the world beyond the nest by tentatively touching nearby twigs and leaves. As the nestlings get bigger, the pliable sides of the nest stretch to fit their growing bodies. They use their feet to anchor themselves to the edge of the nest when they try out their wings for the first time. They beat their wings enthusiastically, an exercise that looks as though they are trying to stand on tiptoe, or dance *en point*.

Mother hummingbirds do not need to push their babies from the nest. The little ones leave of their own accord, eager to try their wings. First flights usually take place in the morning and can be as far as 50 feet (15 m). The young are surprisingly proficient at flying the first time out, but less proficient at landing. It takes a few tries before they successfully gain altitude, and several more to master the aerial acrobatics that are their birthright.

The nestlings normally remain in the nest three weeks, but Ruby-throat nestlings may stay as long as a month. Normally, a hummingbird mother continues to feed and preen her young for almost a month after they have fledged, a total of forty to sixty-five days from hatching. Some researchers have observed a mother hummingbird teaching her young which flowers contain nectar, and how to get it, though in the interest of youthful curiosity and exploration, the young ones try many types of flowers (and some things that aren't flowers) before settling on those that are most rewarding. Mothers also have been observed teaching the young how to use feeders. More often, if the mother continues to feed her young, she will fly to the usual meeting place, and if they are not there, call for them.

Female hummingbirds may raise two or even three broods in a season. They may raise two broods in the same nest, or start a second nest and a second brood while still raising the first. Blue-throated, Allen's, and Anna's Hummingbirds may raise three broods in a season; Ruby-throated, White-eared, and Black-chinned Hummingbirds have been reported to begin building a second nest while still feeding the young in the first. In these cases, the female does double duty: She builds a second nest, mates, and lays eggs, even though she must still guard the first nest and feed the chicks for another two weeks or more. There are also numerous reports of females adopting and feeding chicks that were not their own. Adoption has been observed among several different species in captivity, and among White-eared Hummingbirds in the wild.

Despite the mother's spirited and courageous defense of her nest and chicks, hummingbirds' mortality rates are high, ranging from 25 percent for Allen's to 89 percent for the Andean Hillstar. Less than 50 percent of the chicks of the species studied survived. Studies of fledgling success—from hatching to full feathering—ranged from 17 percent to 59 percent of the number of eggs laid. Predation accounts for most of the nest mortality: Hummingbird mothers fearlessly attack hawks, crows, jays, chipmunks, snakes, and even yellow jackets in defense of the eggs and young, but not always successfully. Accidents and bad weather—high winds, severe cold, heavy rains, and high heat—account for the remainder of fledgling deaths.

Opposite page: Ruby-throated Hummingbird nests resemble a knot on the limb of a tree. Ruby-throats usually choose a small limb that slants downward and saddle the nest over it. The nest is always sheltered by other branches above it and is often directly over a brook. The nest is built mostly of bud scales, lined with down like thistledown, and decorated on the outside with lichens. It is fastened to the limb by spider silk. Incubation for Ruby-throats takes sixteen days, fledging takes from two weeks to four weeks. The mother typically stands on the edge of the nest, bracing her tail against its side, to feed the babies, which she accomplishes by thrusting her entire bill down their throats.

Page 98: This baby Broad-tailed Hummingbird is exercising its wings, practicing flying until the day it actually stands on the edge of the nest and takes off. Hummingbirds are remarkably good fliers from the very beginning, having more difficulty mastering the intricacies of perching than those of flight.

Page 99: This young Broad-tailed Hummingbird is working on the details of balance and grip, both essential to perching. Before long it will have mastered perching and be performing the aerial acrobatics that are its birthright.

THE NORTH
AMERICAN SPECIES

There are 338 species of hummingbirds, not counting four more species that may be hybrids. Sixteen breed within the borders of the continental United States. Fifteen species breed west of the Rocky Mountains, and one east of the Rockies, the Ruby-throated Hummingbird. Most North American species are migrants, breeding in the United States and Canada in warm weather. The exceptions are Anna's Hummingbirds which are resident along the West Coast, Allen's on the Palos Verdes Peninsula in southern California, Costa's, which are resident along the southern California coast, and a few Buff-bellied Hummingbirds in Texas. Migrant hummingbirds begin arriving in the South as early as January or February, and in the North as late as April or May.

The hummingbird descriptions here follow the general pattern of the Peterson Field Identification Method developed by Roger Tory Peterson in his classic "Field Guides" series: The most distinctive identifying feature of each species is listed first. The states through which the birds migrate are listed as they occur along the migratory route from north to south and where states are on a parallel, west to east.

This book is not intended as a field guide, fitting into pockets and packs as poorly as it does, but as a compendium of as much information as is available for each of the sixteen species migratory or resident in North America. Learn which species are likely to be found in your area by reviewing the range maps, then read the description to learn the most distinctive feature of each species so you can identify it. Hang feeders, plant hummingbird flowers, haunt fields of wildflowers, or go on hummingbird safaris to see more hummingbirds. Local chapters of the Audubon Society are an excellent source of local and regional information. They can also tell you of any rare or unusual species that turn up in your area, and where to go to see them.

Hummingbirds are flower pollinators, and many North American flowers are adapted to hummingbird pollination. The flowers hummingbirds feed on are listed with each species with a common name and the scientific name in all cases where both are known. Where only one or the other is known, it is listed singly. On page 130 there is an additional list of garden plants that hummingbirds are attracted to. The flowers with each species are intended to help the birder find hummingbirds of that particular species. Some of the plants included are native to Central or South America.

Where do you find hummingbirds? Simply look for the flowers they feed on.

Allen's Hummingbird

Species: SELASPHORUS SASIN

© H. Clarke/VIREO

Other Names: Red-backed Hummingbird; Chupamirto petirrojo (Spanish). Named for Charles Andrew Allen (1841–1930) of Milton, Massachusetts, who collected it in California. Named *Selasphorus alleni* in his honor, the bird was later discovered to be a specimen of the species previously named *Selasphorus sasin*. The original name took precedence *(Selasphorus* is Latin, *sasin* is the Nootka Indian word for the hummingbird)*, but Allen's name lives on in the common English name.

Size: 3¹/₂ to 3³/₄ inches (8.75–9.4 cm).

Field Marks:

MALE: Rufous sides, rump, tail, and cheeks; glittering orange-red throat; green back. The all-green back distinguishes it from the Rufous, which has a mostly rufous back. The Allen's male makes a whistling sound with its wings in flight.

FEMALE: Mostly a metallic bronze-green with a little rufous on the upper part of the tail. Cannot be distinguished from female Rufous *(Selasphorus rufus)* in the field.

Range: Along the coast of California and in northwestern Mexico, occasionally in Arizona, Oregon, and Washington. Breeds in coastal California from San Clemente and the Santa Catalina Islands north to Eureka. Winters from southern California to central Baja California and Chihuahua, Mexico.

Migration: Migratory only at northern end of range. Spring migration is from January to March. Migrates south from July through August. One species, *S.s. sedentarius*, is resident on Palos Verdes Peninsula and the Channel Islands in southern California. Migrants pass through mountains of central southern Arizona in July and August en route to central Mexico. Adult males precede females by two weeks, immature males by a month. The migratory route is elliptical, north along the coast in the spring, south along the foothills of the Sierra Nevada in autumn.

Nesting Season: Early February to late June. Peak is mid-March to late May.

Habitat: Canyon woodlands and brush; mountain meadows. Feeds from California fuchsia *(Zauschneria californica* var. *latifolia)*, California lilac *(Ceanothus* spp.*)*, century plant flower stalks *(Agave* spp.*)*, columbines *(Aquilegia* spp.*)*, hedge-nettles *(Stachys albens)*, honeysuckle *(Lonicera involucrata ledebourii)*, Indian paintbrush *(Castilleja* spp.*)*, madrone *(Arbutus menziesii)*, monkey flowers *(Mimulus guttatus* and *M. cardinalis* as well as *Diplacus* spp.*)*, scarlet sage *(Salvia* spp.*)*, tree tobacco *(Nicotiana glauca)*, and many garden plants.

Anna's Hummingbird

© P. Pyle/VIREO

Species: CALYPTE ANNA, ARCHILOCHUS ANNA (LESSON)

Other Names: The English name comes from the Latin binomial. Also Chupamirto cuello escarlata (Spanish). Named for the lovely Anna de Belle Massena, wife of François Victor Massena, Duke of Rivoli, a French nobleman who collected stuffed hummingbird specimens in the 1800s. (Massena's collection, one of the largest private collections of stuffed birds of the nineteenth century, was acquired by the Academy of Natural Sciences in Philadelphia in 1846.)

Size: 3½ to 4 inches (9.75–10 cm).

Field Marks:
The largest California hummingbird, and the only one found in California in midwinter. MALE: Brilliant rose red helmet (can flash gold or violet), red throat, emerald-green back, gray underparts. Only hummingbird in the United States with a red crown. FEMALE: Crimson patch at throat, emerald-green back and sides, gray underparts. Bigger and grayer below than the Costa's *(Calypte costae)* female, chunkier than the female Black-chinned Hummingbird *(Archilochus alexandri).*

Range: California and Baja California. One of the few hummingbirds resident in North America, the Anna's is expanding its range north, south, and east. It has been reported in Alaska, British Columbia, Washington, Oregon, Montana, Colorado, Nevada, New Mexico, and Texas.

Migration: Doesn't really migrate, although small numbers move into southern Arizona in September, and leave in December.

Nesting Season: One of the earliest breeding birds in North America. Breeds from mid-December to mid-August.

Habitat: Mixed woodland or chaparral, canyons, and gardens. Feeds from century plant *(Agave americana)*, currants *(Ribes malvaceus* and *R. speciosum)*, Eucalyptus trees *(Eucalyptus* spp.*)*, Indian paintbrush *(Castilleja martinii,* and *C. foliosa)*, Indian pink *(Silene laciniata)*, manzanita *(Arctostaphylos glauca)*, monkey flower *(Mimulus* and *Diplacus* spp.*)*, tree tobacco *(Nicotiana glauca)*, and many garden plants, particularly red-hot poker *(Knipfolia uvaria)*. It hawks midges on the wing, and visits sapsucker wells for both the sap and the insects attracted to the sap.

Berylline Hummingbird

Species: AMAZILIA BERYLLINA

Other Names: Chupaflor de berilo; Chupaflor colicanelo (Spanish).

Size: 3½ inches (9 cm).

Field Marks:
MALE: Brilliant green underparts, head, throat, and back; rufous-brown wings; rufous rump and tail. Upper bill is black, lower half red.
FEMALE: Brilliant green back, gray or brown underparts. Otherwise, similar to male.

Range: Southeast Arizona; Sonora, and Chihuahua, south to Chiapas and east to Veracruz in Mexico, as well as Guatemala, El Salvador, and Honduras.

Migration: The rarest of the North American hummingbirds. Probably migratory only at the northern edge of its range. First recorded in 1967. The few United States records are all from Arizona from late June to September, mostly Ramsey Canyon, Cave Creek, and Carr Canyon in the Huachuca Mountains, as well as the Santa Rita Mountains, and Chiricahua Mountains. In Mexico, it is resident, migrating vertically from lower altitudes to higher.

Nesting Season: July to September. Nests are camouflaged with lichens, and have a streamer of grass blades attached to the bottom with spider web. Nests in the United States in Arizona sycamore *(Plantanus wrightii)*, in Mexico in *Wigandia caracasana*, pines *(Pinus* spp.*)*, firs *(Abies* spp.*)*, oaks *(Quercus* spp.*)*, and flowering shrubs.

Habitat: Riparian canyons at 5,392 to 5,682 feet (1,617–1,704 m) in the United States. In Mexico, in mountain woodlands between 2,970 to 9,900 feet (891–2,970 m), in dense pine *(Pinus* spp.*)*, pine-oak or fir *(Abies* spp.*)* forest, and suburban gardens. In Colima, Mexico, where it is common, its habitat includes the thorn forest, deciduous tropical forest, oak *(Quercus* spp.*)* woodlands, and both arid and humid pine-oak forests. Feeds from *Calliandra anomala, Ceiba aesculifolia, Lemairocereus, Psittacanthus calyculatus,* and Turk's-head *(Malaviscus arboreus)*.

© Michael H. Francis/The Wildlife Collection

Black-chinned Hummingbird

Species: ARCHILOCHUS ALEXANDRI

Other Names: Purple-throated Hummingbird, Terciopelo barbanegro (Spanish).

Size: 3¹/₃ to 3³/₄ inches (8–9 cm).

Field Marks:
MALE: Black chin, white collar, violet band between chin and collar, green back, purple-bronze tail, gray underparts.
FEMALE: Green back, whitish underparts, bronze-green upper tail, black lower tail with white tips on outside feathers, a gray-brown forehead and crown. May be confused with Anna's *(Calypte Anna)*, Costa's *(Calypte costae)*, and Ruby-throat females *(Archilochus colubris)* where ranges overlap. It's smaller than the Anna's, has less green in the tail feathers than the Costa's, and has less green on the crown and a shorter bill than the Ruby-throat.

Range: Western North America.

Migration: Winters in southern California, southern Guerrero and the Federal District of Mexico. Breeds in British Columbia, Washington, Oregon, California, Montana, Idaho, Colorado, New Mexico, Texas, southern Chihuahua, southern Sonora, and northeastern Baja California. It is the most common nesting hummingbird in Texas. The sexes migrate separately, the males arriving first.

Nesting Season: April to September; peak is May to June. Males display a series of long 100-foot (30-m) swoops, moving to and fro like a pendulum; the bottom of the arc is just over the female's head. The swoop may also be a long, narrow figure eight, accompanied by a loud whistling sound, made by the wings or tail feathers. The male may hover at each end of the arc and call, or clap his wings together underneath himself to make a sound similar to that of a bird bathing.

Habitat: Canyons, chaparral, streambed groves. Nests found in alders *(Alnus* spp.*)*, cottonwoods *(Populus* spp.*)*, sycamores *(Platanus* spp.*)*, valley oaks *(Quercus lobata)*, and willows *(Salix* spp.*)*. Males frequent drier canyons with live oaks *(Quercus agrifolia, Q. chrysolepis, Q. wislizenii)* or desert washes with mesquite *(Prosopis glandulosa)*, and catclaw *(Acacia greggii)*. In Texas, Black-chinned Hummingbirds are found in agave-cactus *(Agave* spp., *Cactacaea* spp.*)* desert and juniper-oak woods *(Juniperus* spp., *Quercus,* spp.*)*. They feed from flowers of agave *(Agave* spp.*)*, buckeye *(Aesculus* spp.*)*, butterfly bush *(Buddleia* spp.*)*, citrus trees *(Citrus* spp.*)*, desert honeysuckle *(Anisacanthus thurberi)*, ironwood *(Cercocarpus* spp.*)*, Japanese honeysuckle *(Lonicera japonica)*, lantana *(Lantana* spp.*)*, *Lycium andersoni*, mountain laurel *(Kalmia latifolia?)*, nasturtium *(Tropaeolum majus)*, ocotillo *(Fouqueria splendens)*, palo verde *(Cercidium* spp.*)*, red larkspur *(Delphinium cardinalis)*, shrimp plant *(Justicia brandegeana)*, Texas redbud *(Cercis reniformis?)*, and tree tobacco *(Nicotiana glauca)* among others.

Blue-throated Hummingbird

Species: LAMPORNIS CLEMENCIAE

Other Names: Chupamirto garganta azul (Spanish).

Size: 4^1/$_2$ to 5^1/$_2$ inches (11.25–13.75 cm).

Field Marks:
The largest of the hummingbirds found in North America.
MALE: Large tail with big white patches, light blue throat, white eyestripe, gray-green crown, dull bronze-green body, slate gray underparts.
FEMALE: Large tail with big white patches, gray underparts, white eyestripe and white "whisker" on face, dull green body.

Range: Arizona, New Mexico, Texas (Chisos Mountains), Guerrero and Michoacan, Mexico.

Migration: Breeds in Arizona, New Mexico, Texas, and Nuevo Leon, Mexico; winters in Guerrero and Michoacan, Mexico. In the United States from April to July. Migrates north between March and May, south between August and October.

Nesting Season: April to July in Arizona; varies considerably in Mexico. Female Blue-throats seek out sheltered nesting sites to a greater degree than any other North American hummingbird, preferring rock overhangs, vertical canyon walls, and under the eaves of old barns and bunkhouses. One nest in Ramsey Canyon, Arizona, was used ten years in succession by a female who produced up to three broods per season in it. The nest measured 5 inches (12.5 cm) high by 2^1/$_2$ inches (6.25 cm) in diameter. When collected, it was estimated that the nest contained 15,000 miles (24,000 km) of spider web and caterpillar silk. The female, seeing her nest of ten years gone, immediately began building a new one. The old nest was taken June 24; the new one had two eggs in it by July 10. It takes the female from fifteen to thirty days to construct a new nest. The nests are supported from one side or the rim, with the opening at the side. Dry oak catkins, moss, straw, stems, and lichens are used to build and decorate the nest.

Habitat: Wooded streams of mountain canyons where the vegetation is lush. In the Chisos Mountains of Texas at elevations of 5,000 to 7,500 feet (1,500–2,250 m) among bigtooth maples *(Acer saccharum grandidentatum)*, cypress *(Cupressus arizonica)*, oaks *(Quercus* spp.*)*, and pine *(Pinus* spp.*)*. Also found in the Huachuca and Chiricahua Mountains of Arizona where it feeds from agave *(Agave* spp.*)*, gilia *(Gilia subnuda)*, *Lamourouxia exerta*, *Lobelia laxiflora*, *Penstemon kunthii*, pineapple sage *(Salvia elegans)*, purple penstemon *(Penstemon campanulatus)*, other sages *(Salvia cardinalis, S. genaereflora)*, shrubby honeysuckle *(Lonicera arizonica)*, and tree tobacco *(Nicotiana glauca)*. Insects and spiders dominate its diet in the summer, including daddy longlegs, small beetles, flies, and wasps.

Broad-billed Hummingbird

Species: CYNANTHUS LATIROSTRIS

Other Names: Chuparrosa matraquita; Chupaflor piquancho (Spanish).

Size: 3¼ to 4 inches (8.75–10 cm).

Field Marks:
A dark bird; may look black at a distance.
MALE: Large, iridescent, dark blue-green throat; bright red bill with black tip; emerald-green back, sides, and breast; white underparts.
FEMALE: Bright red bill with black tip, pearl-gray throat patch, grey underparts, thin white eyestripe, bronze-green tail.

Range: Texas to southern Arizona to central Mexico.

Migration: Breeds in the United States in southeast Arizona, southwest New Mexico, and western Texas. Winters in northern and central Mexico. Migrates north March to April, south September to October. The Broad-billed Hummingbird is migratory in the United States, resident in Mexico.

Nesting Season: Breeds mid-April to August in the United States, January to May in Mexico. Almost nothing is known of the display behavior of Broad-billed Hummingbirds. The male display consists of a pendulum-like swing back and forth in front of the female, accompanied by a sound like the zing of a rifle bullet.

Nothing is known of brooding behavior, incubation periods, or fledging periods. Nests are very small with an inside diameter of only ¾ inch (1.8 cm), woven of grass stalks, lined with plant down, and camouflaged with bits of bark and dead leaves; they mimic the little balls of dead vegetation caught in streamside branches when the water is high. Nests are found in apricot trees *(Prunus armeniacas),* espino *(thorn)* trees, hackberry trees *(Celtis pallida, C. reticulata, C. douglasii),* mesquite *(Prosopsis glandulosa),* sycamores *(Platanus* spp.*),* willows *(Salix* spp.*),* and in vine-covered bushes and on vines.

Habitat: Arid mountain canyons with streams or springs and mesquite-sycamore *(Platanus* spp.*)* groves in the United States. Feeds from agave *(Agave* spp.*),* ocotillos *(Fouqueria splendens),* penstemon *(Penstemon* spp.*),* and other flowers. The diet also includes leafhoppers, aphids, root gnats, flower flies, spiders, daddy longlegs, and other bugs. Not much research has been done on its foraging habits.

Broad-tailed Hummingbird

Species: SELASPHORUS PLATYCERCUS

Other Names: Chupamirto cola ancha (Spanish).

Size: 4 to 4½ inches (10–11.25 cm).

Field Marks:
The male is the only hummingbird in the West with a red throat and green crown. Wings make a distinctive musical trill, like the song of small crickets.
MALE: Brilliant red throat; emerald-green crown, back, and tail. Similar to Ruby-throat *(Archilochus colubris)*, but ranges don't overlap.
FEMALE: Bronze-green back and sides, white chin and throat, grayish white chest and underparts, rufous sides and flanks. Impossible to identify in the field because range overlaps with Allen's, Rufous, Costa's, Calliope, and Black-chinned, and all the females are distressingly similar in coloration. The Broad-tailed female's tail is unusually large, and the female is also large by comparison with the others.

Range: Western United States and Central America.

Migration: Breeds in mountains of eastern-central California, northern Nevada, northern Wyoming, eastern Colorado, New Mexico, and southwestern Texas in the United States. Also found in southern Mexico and highlands of Guatemala. Winters in south-central Mexico. Migrates north March to May, south August to October.

Nesting Season: Breeds in the United States March to July. Males perform a 30- to 40-foot (9–12-m) U-shaped dive display, accompanied by a musical buzzing from the wings and a clicking noise made at the bottom of the arc. A similar courtship display, performed over the head of a perched female, consists of a 30- to 50-foot (9–15-m) U-shaped dive. The bottom of the arc passes just over her head. The musical buzzing that accompanies the flight of the Broad-tailed as a result of the slotted primaries on the wings is louder than usual during the courtship display. There may also be sharp, clicking notes during the dive or three "flups" at the bottom of the dive produced by the wings or tail. Sometimes the male and female hover nearly bill-to-bill in the air. On one occasion, three males displayed together, the only known instance of a lek (a group of males displaying courtship behavior) in the United States. The few observed copulations took place while the female was perched. After coition the female preens extensively.

The nesting season lasts thirty-eight to sixty-four days. Females may raise two broods simultaneously. Females often build nests in the same place year after year. Nests may be on large limbs or on twigs. The Broad-tailed female nests in alders *(Alnus* spp.*)*, aspen and cottonwoods *(Populus* spp.*)*, fir *(Abies* spp.*)*, pines *(Pinus* spp.*)*, spruce *(Picea* spp.*)*, sycamores *(Platanus* spp.*)*, and willows *(Salix* spp.*)* 3 to 13 feet (1–4 m) in the air, and often on branches that stretch out over water. The nests are camouflaged with lichens, shreds of bark, leaves, and other plant materials. Because the Broad-tailed is a bird of the high mountains, it is often exposed to low temperatures. On nights following rainy days, the female usually becomes torpid, and nest temperature drops dramatically from 90° to 52°F (32° to 11°C) or even lower, but this does not seem to harm the eggs or nestlings.

Habitat: Mountain meadows adjoining coniferous forests. In California, they are found in mixed pine woodlands with thickets of willow or silk-tassel bush *(Garrya spp.)* near streambeds. In Colorado, in moist canyons during the breeding season, later moving to timberline and alpine meadows thick with flowers. In Texas, in pine-oak woodlands or in scrub junipers *(Juniperus* spp.*)* on slopes or in canyons. During migration, in the foothills and open valleys. Feeds from agaves *(Agave* spp.*)*, certain cacti *(Echinocereus triglochidiatus)*, figworts *(Scrophularia spp.)*, gilia *(Ipomopsis aggregata)*, gooseberries *(Ribes* spp.*)*, larkspur *(Delphinium nelsoni, D. barbeyi)*, locusts *(Robinia neomexicana* and other *Robinia spp.)*, lupines *(Lupinus spp.)*, paintbrush *(Castilleja miniata)*, penstemon *(Penstemon barbatus)*, sage *(Salvia spp.)*, western blue flag *(Iris missouriensis)*, willow catkins *(Salix spp.)*, and yuccas *(Yucca spp.)*.

Buff-bellied Hummingbird

Species: AMAZILIA YUCATANENSIS

Other Names: Fawn-breasted Hummingbird; Yucatán Hummingbird. Chupamirto yucateco; Chupaflor vientre castano (Spanish).

Size: 4 to 4½ inches (10–11.25 cm).

Field Marks:
The only red-billed green hummingbird in the United States.
MALE AND FEMALE: Green crown, iridescent green throat, green back, buff belly, slightly forked rufous tail with chestnut tips, red bill.

Range: Gulf Coast regions of southern Texas, eastern Mexico (Yucatán Peninsula), and Belize.

Migration: North from June to July after breeding, south from August. Relatively sedentary in most of its range, resident year-round in Texas along the coast.

Nesting Season: Late March to mid-July; peak is May to June. There were once far more Buff-bellied Hummingbirds breeding in Texas than there are now. Nothing is known of the Buff-bellied's courtship/threat displays, brooding periods, brooding behavior, incubation periods or behavior.

Nests are built near woodland paths or roads, 3 to 10 feet (.9–3 m) off the ground. The nests are saddled on small limbs or twigs of anachita *(Cordia boissieri)*, Texas ebony *(Pithecellobium flexicaule)*, hackberry *(Celtis* spp.*)*, and willows *(Salix* spp.*)*, and woven of plant fibers, lined with thistledown, and distinctively decorated with flowers, bits of bark, and light-colored lichens. The nest is 1.6 inches (4 cm) wide, 1.3 inches (3.25 cm) deep; the cup is not quite 1 inch (2.5 cm) wide and about ½ inch (1.25 cm) deep. The nest may be used season after season, built higher each time.

Habitat: Dense thickets of flowering bushes and creeping vines along streams, gullies, and even the coast in Texas. Semiarid coastal scrub in Mexico, high deciduous forest and rain forest in Belize. Known to feed from anaqua *(Ehretia anacua)*, giant Turk's cap *(Malvaviscus grandiflorus)*, mesquite *(Prosopsis glandulosa)*, and Texas ebony *(Pithecellobium flexicaule)*.

Calliope Hummingbird

Species: STELLULA CALLIOPE (ARCHILOCHUS CALLIOPE)

Other Names: Chupamirto rafaguitas (Spanish).

Size: 2³/₄ to 3¹/₂ inches (7–8.75 cm).

Field Marks:

The smallest hummingbird in North America.

MALE: Streaks of brilliant red-purple-magenta *(solferino)* across the white throat, gold-green back, brownish gray tail. No other hummingbird has a red-and-white striped gorget.

FEMALE: The tiniest bird in North America; her size and short bill are the best field marks. Otherwise, very similar in coloration to Rufous, Black-chinned, and Broad-tailed females—mostly green with some rufous. Hovering is distinctive in both sexes: The tail is still and held unusually high above the plane of the body.

Range: Western North American (except Southwest and West Coast) and Mexico.

Migration: North from March to May, south from late July to September. Breeds in British Columbia, southwestern Alberta, Washington, Idaho, Montana, Oregon, Wyoming, California, Nevada, Utah, and Baja California. Winters in Michoacan, Mexico (D.F.), and Guerrero, Mexico. Migratory route is oval, like the Allen's and Rufous Hummingbirds, but narrower. Route is closer to the Pacific coast in the spring going north, closer to the mountains in autumn headed south. In autumn the males migrate a week before the females and immatures.

Nesting Season: May to July; peaks in June. The male displays in U-shaped arcs 60 to 90 feet (18–27 m) high and 23 to 27 feet (7–8 m) wide. Its wings buzz as it flies and it makes an explosive "zing" at the bottom of the arc near the female. Coition is performed perching.

The nests are often in conifers in clusters of old cones. In aspens *(Populus* spp.*)*, the nests mimic knots of mistletoe. Typical nesting trees include alder *(Alnus* spp.*)*, alpine fir *(Abies lasiocarpa)*, arborvitae *(Thuja occidentalis)*, Douglas fir *(Pseudotsuga menziesii)*, Englemann spruce *(Picea engelmannii)*, pine *(Pinus ponderosa)*, silver fir *(Abies amabilis)*, and western hemlock *(Tsuga heterophylla)*. Nests are usually 3 to 15 feet (.9–4.5 m) above the ground. Nests may be oriented to catch the first rays of the rising sun, or under overhanging branches for extra warmth. Nests are built of moss, needles, bark, and leaves, all bound together with spider web and lined with the soft fiber of willows *(Salix* spp.*)* or cottonwoods *(Populus* spp.*)*. The same nesting places are used year after year, one nest piled on top of the one before, some to four stories in height. No one knows how long it takes the female to build the nest, which is 1¹/₄ to 1³/₄ inches (3.1–4.9 cm) in diameter. The Calliope continues to build her nest long after the young are hatched.

Incubation is about fifteen days, the nestling phase is eighteen to twenty-three days; nobody knows the duration of the fledgling phase, and the female raises only one brood. Despite the cold temperatures in the high mountains, the females do not become torpid at night.

Habitat: Wooded canyons, alpine meadows, open grasslands. Calliopes feed from columbine *(Aquilegia formosa)*, currants and gooseberries *(Ribes spp.)*, Indian paintbrush *(Castilleja spp.)*, lousewort *(Pedicularis semibarbata)*, manzanitas *(Arctostaphylos spp.)*, penstemon *(Penstemon menziesii davidsonii, P. newberryi)*, sage *(Salvia spp.)*, scarlet gilia *(Ipomopsis rubra)*, snow plant *(Sarcodes sanguinea)*, willows *(Salix spp.)*, and yellow monkey flower *(Mimulus tilingii)* among others. They also hawk insects in flight.

The Calliope has an exceptionally wide vertical range, from as low as the Columbia River Valley to just below the timberline in the Sierra Nevada—from 600 to 8,000 feet (180–2,400 m).

Costa's Hummingbird

Species: CALYPTE COSTAE

Other Names: Coast Hummingbird, Ruffed Hummingbird. Chupamirto garganta violeta (Spanish).

Size: 3 to 3½ inches (7.5–8.75 cm).

Field Marks:
The male is the only North American hummingbird with a purple crown and gorget feathers that stick out along the side.
MALE: Full amethyst-purple helmet, head, and throat; gorget feathers extend out to the side; green back, green tail, grayish underparts.
FEMALE: Spots of purple on the throat; mostly green with pale underparts; otherwise, impossible to distinguish from Black-chinned *(Archilochus alexandri)* female in the field.

Range: Southwestern United States and Mexico.

Migration: Costa's Hummingbirds make comparatively short migrations. Breeds in California, southern Nevada, southwestern Utah, Arizona, and New Mexico, as well as southern Baja California and central Mexico. Winters in Arizona, California, Baja California, and western mainland Mexico.

Nesting Season: In the Palos Verdes Peninsula in California, where it is resident, breeding takes place as early as December, one of the earliest breeding seasons known for any North American bird. Ordinarily, however, the breeding season is February to August, and a Costa's female may raise two broods. Males display in a large oval. In *Hummingbirds of North America,* Paul Johnsgard says the display is accompanied by a sound reported as sounding like "the shriek of a glancing bullet." Other flight displays include a slow, short, swinging shuttle flight about 3 feet (.9 m) long, and a narrower U-shaped arc, with steeper dives, accompanied by a booming noise. The Costa's male (the accosting male?) approaches the female from the front, making short darting flights toward her from various angles. If she sits still for this, he mounts her as she perches, then flies off, and again darts at her, at which point they take off in close pursuit.

Nests average 1½ inches (3.75 cm) in outside diameter. Some sixteen different trees are listed as nesting sites as well as cholla cacti *(Opuntia),* sage *(Salvia* spp.*),* yucca *(Yucca* spp.*),* and other cacti, and plants identified in the scientific literature as "other weeds." Nests have also been found in citrus trees in orchards, on vines clinging to rock faces, and in palms.

Habitat: Hot desert areas, chaparral, and woodlands. Often in desert washes, mesas, and hillsides. It feeds from cholla cacti *(Opuntia),* chuparosa *(Anisacanthus thurberi),* mesquite *(Prosopis glandulosa),* ocotillo *(Fouqueria splendens),* sages *(Salvia* spp.*),* yucca *(Yucca* spp.*),* and other flowering plants. The Costa's goes without water longer than any other North American hummingbird.

Lucifer Hummingbird

Species: CALOTHORAX LUCIFER

Other Names: Chupamirto morada grande (Spanish).

Size: 3³/₄ inches (9.4 cm).

Field Marks:
The Lucifer is the only North American hummingbird with a long down-curved bill.
MALE: Iridescent amethyst-purple throat with feathers that extend out to the side, rusty sides, gray-green crown, green back, greenish brown *forked* tail.
FEMALE: Buffy underparts, *rounded* greenish brown tail, green back.

Range: Arizona, New Mexico, and Texas to central Mexico.

Migration: North in April to May, south in September. Breeds in southeastern Arizona, New Mexico, and western Texas; winters in Jalisco, Guerrero, east to Puebla, Mexico. Males precede females by a few days, sometimes arriving as early as March.

Nesting Season: June to July. Two types of display flights have been observed. The first is performed daily, and early in the morning, by the male. He shuttles between two horizontal perches, then spirals upward, dives again at top speed to one of the perches. The second display begins with a male performing for a perched female. He spirals upward to a height of 66 feet (20 m), hovers momentarily, then dives toward the female, pulling out of the dive while still well above her, and drifting slowly down to her in a series smaller and smaller pendulumlike swings. The male then flies upward again.

Nests have been found in agave flower stalks *(Agave lechuguilla)*, and shrubs 3¹/₂ to 13 feet (1–4 m) above the ground. The nests are built of grass seeds, bits of leaves, and plant fibers, lined with plant down, and decorated with small leaves. Almost nothing is known of incubation or brooding behavior, or the length of time incubation and brooding require.

Habitat: Open deserts and arid slopes. The Lucifer tends to be found in the open desert in the spring when flowers are blooming, then moves to higher elevations in the summer. In the United States, it is closely associated with *Agave lechuguilla*, but feeds from other agaves *(Agave americana, A. chisoensis, A. havariana)*, cacti *(Opuntia* spp.*)*, candelilla *(Euphorbia antisyphilitica)*, catclaw *(Acacia greggii)*, Chiso bluebonnet *(Lupinus havardii)*, coral trees *(Erythrina corallodendrum, E. coralloides)*, eucalypts *(Eucalyptus* spp.*)*, *Loesalia mexicana*, lupine *(Lupinus elegans)*, mormon tea *(Ephedra* spp.*)*, ocotillo *(Fouqueria splendens)*, sage *(Salvia mexicana)*, sotal *(Dasylirion leiophyllum)*, tree tobacco *(Nicotiana glauca)*, and yucca *(Yucca* spp.*)*. The few studies that have been done suggest that an unusually high percentage of the Lucifer's diet is insects. The insects are probably found in flowers since the down-curved bill is ill-suited to hawking insects on the wing.

Magnificent Hummingbird

© Wendy Shattil/Bob Rosinski

Species: EUGENES FULGENS, HELIODOXA FULGENS (Swainson)

Other Names: Rivoli's Hummingbird; Chupamirto verde montero; chupaflor magnifico (Spanish).

Size: 4¹/₂ to 5 inches (11.25–12.5 cm).

Field Marks:
Large for a hummingbird; looks all black at a distance.
MALE: Blackish belly, emerald-green throat (may flash gold or blue, depending on angle to light), brilliant royal purple crown, golden green back, green tail with a bit of gray.
FEMALE: Greenish above, pale underparts, golden green head, back, and tail; white eye stripe.

Range: Arizona, New Mexico, and Texas south to Panama.

Migration: North in April, south in October and November. In the United States it breeds in western Colorado, Arizona, New Mexico, and Texas. It winters in Mexico, Guatemala, El Salvador, and Nicaragua. In Mexico the resident birds may not be migratory, except vertically, moving only between the valleys and the mountains.

Nesting Season: May to July. Nothing is known of courtship, mating, incubation, or brooding behavior for the Magnificent Hummingbird.

The nests are found in alder *(Alnus* spp.*)*, cottonwoods *(Populus* spp.*)*, Douglas fir *(Pseudotsuga menziesii)*, pine *(Pinus* spp.*)*, Rocky Mountain maple *(Acer glabrum)*, sycamore *(Platanus* spp.*)*, and walnut *(Juglans major [J. rupestris* var. *major])*. The nests are typically saddled on small, horizontal branches smaller in diameter than the nests themselves. Nests are made of mosses and other soft plants, lined with plant down or feathers, and decorated so heavily on the outside with lichens that they appear to be shingled with them. It takes the female a week to build a nest and lay her two eggs. The nests are found anywhere from 10 to 53 feet (3 to 16 m) above the ground.

Habitat: Mountain canyons, forest edges, and wooded streams. In Arizona it is found in the Huachaca and Chiricahua Mountains on the edges of ponderosa pine forest, sometimes as high as the fir zone. It is also frequently found at the lower edge of the pine belt around flowering agaves *(Agave* spp.*)*, honeysuckle *(Lonicera involucrata)*, and penstemon *(Penstemon* spp.*)*. In New Mexico it is found in the San Luis Mountains from the fir zone to canyon bottoms with streams, and in Texas in the Chisos Mountains in mixed woodlands of juniper *(Juniperus* spp.*)*, oak *(Quercus* spp.*)*, and pine *(Pinus* spp.*)*. Magnificent Hummingbirds feed from agave *(Agave americana, A. parryi)*, *Bomarea costaricenensis, Centropogon talamenensis*, coral trees *(Erythrina corallodendrum)*, *Fuchsia splendens*, honeysuckle *(Lonicera* spp.*)*, iris *(Iris* spp.*)*, *Lobelia laxiflora*, penstemon *(Penstemon bicolor, P. kunthii)*, scarlet geraniums *(Pelargonium* spp.*)*, scarlet salvia *(Salvia* spp.*)*, and thistles *(Cirsium* spp.*)*.

Ruby-throated Hummingbird

Species: ARCHILOCHUS COLUBRIS (LINNAEUS)

Other Names: Chupaflor rubi; Mansoncito garganta de fuego (Spanish).

Size: 3 to 3¾ inches (7.5–9.4 cm).

Field Marks:
The only hummingbird that breeds east of the Rockies.
MALE: Brilliant ruby throat, green back, dark *forked* tail, grayish white underparts, and green head.
FEMALE: Dark, *rounded* tail with white spots, otherwise iridescent green with pale underparts.

Range: Breeds in Alberta, Saskatchewan, Manitoba, Ontario, Quebec, New Brunswick, and Nova Scotia in Canada. In the United States, breeds in all the states east of the Rocky Mountains. Winters in southern Florida and southern Texas, and south through Mexico and Central America to Panama.

Migration: North from late February to mid-May; south from late July to late October. The Ruby-throated Hummingbird migrates from its wintering grounds in Central and South America by flying nonstop over the Gulf of Mexico. For many years, scientists could not figure out how it did it, and some even postulated routes that involved rest stops on various islands in the Caribbean. It has since been established that birds with .07 ounce (2 g) of fat have sufficient energy reserves to fly 650 miles (1,050 km), more than enough to get them the 500 miles (800 km) across the Gulf. A few Ruby-throats winter in coastal Texas. Their arrival in their northern breeding grounds coincides with the blooming of important food flowers such as buffalo currant (*Ribes odoratum*), columbine (*Aquilegia canadensis*), and horse chestnut (Texas buckeye, *Aesculus pavia*). In the northeastern states, nine hummingbird food species are in bloom by May, and by the time the flowers have stopped blooming in October, the Ruby-throat is already headed south.

Nesting Season: March to mid-June. Males arrive earlier than the females. The males' dive display describes a wide, shallow arc 10 to 15 feet (3 to 4.5 m) in the air. The male flies back and forth as though suspended from a string, describing a perfect arc. The male "buzzes" the perched female with his wings at the bottom of the arc; the loud "buzz" is made with its tail and wings. In another flight display, the male and female hover in the air 1 or 2 feet (.3–.6 m) apart, facing each other, flying straight up and down. They also perform a shuttle flight, with short, fast zips back and forth. One observed coition took place on the ground following a display flight.

The female builds the nest mostly of bud scales or small leaves securely lashed to the branch with spider web, lined with plant down, and covered on the outside with lichens. More lining may be added while she incubates the eggs. The nest is 1 inch

(2.5 cm) wide and 1 inch (2.5 cm) deep, and takes the female a week to ten days to build. The nest is always sheltered by overhanging limbs, often built on a branch that stretches out over water, and resembles a small knot on the branch. Nests are usually 5 to 20 feet (1.5–6 m) up in the tree. They are built in hickories *(Juglandaceae* spp.*)*, hornbeams *(Carpinus caroliniana)*, junipers *(Juniperus* spp.*)*, pines *(Pinus* spp.*)*, lichen-covered post oaks *(Quercus minor)*, sweet gum *(Liquidambar styraciflua)*, and tulip-poplars *(Liriodendron tulipifera)*, located at the edge of a meadow, on the bank of a stream, or near a road. Sometimes the birds use old nests again, for a second brood the same season, or in subsequent years. Incubation takes sixteen days, fledging from two to three weeks.

Habitat: Woods, gardens, and orchards. The Ruby-throat feeds from, and pollinates, at least thirty-one native plant species in eastern North America, as well as many more introduced and cultivated species. They are attracted to bee balm or Oswego tea *(Monarda didyma)*, cardinal flower *(Lobelia cardinalis)*, jewelweed *(Impatiens* spp.*)*, and spotted touch-me-not *(Impatiens capensis, I. pallida)*. In the garden they feed on azaleas *(Rhododendron* spp.*)*, busy lizzie *(Impatiens wallerana,* includes *I. holstii* and *I. sultanii)*, butterfly bush *(Buddleia* spp.*)*, foxglove *(Digitalis* spp.*)*, honeysuckle *(Lonicera* spp.*)*, larkspur *(Delphinium* spp.*)*, lilies *(Lilium* spp.*)*, lupine *(Lupinus* spp.*)*, penstemon *(Penstemon* spp.*)*, quince *(Chaenomeles)*, and weigela *(Weigela* spp.*)*.

In the northernmost part of its range, the Ruby-throat may arrive before the earliest plants are in bloom; sometimes it survives on insects alone. Other times it robs the sap wells of sapsuckers (particularly the yellow-bellied sapsucker, which ranges farthest north of the four sapsucker species). It eats the sap and whatever small insects have been attracted by the sap's sweetness as well. The Ruby-throat may find the wells by following the sapsuckers, since Ruby-throats have been seen following sapsuckers from tree to tree. It is possible that the northernmost range of the Ruby-throat in the east and the Rufous Hummingbird in the west is determined, not entirely by the availability of flower nectar, but in some part by the presence of sapsuckers and their wells.

© T.J. Cawley/Tom Stack & Associates

Rufous Hummingbird

Species: SELASPHORUS RUFUS

Other Names: Chupamirto dorada (Spanish).

Size: 3¹/₃ to 3⁷/₈ inches (8.25–9.75 cm).

Field Marks:
The male is the only North American hummingbird with a rufous back.
MALE: Rufous back, sides, and tail (the back may be flecked with green, and the very similar male Allen's Hummingbird *(Selasphorus sasin)* also has a green back). The throat flashes orange-red and copper. The bird has a white breast, bright reddish brown underparts, and a rufous tail with black tips.
FEMALE: Green back, rufous sides and tail, flecks of iridescent red on throat, white-tipped tail. Indistinguishable from the Allen's *(Selasphorus sasin)* female in the field.

Range: Ranges farthest north of all the North American hummingbirds, well into southeastern Alaska. In the United States, breeds in Alaska, Washington, Idaho, western Montana, Oregon, northwest Wyoming, and along the northern California coast; in Canada, breeds in southern Yukon, British Columbia, and western Alberta. Winters in Jalisco, Michoacan, and Zacatecas, Mexico.

Migration: The Rufous Hummingbird has the longest migration of all the North American hummingbirds, 2,500 miles (4,000 km) going north, as much as 3,500 miles (5,600 km) going south—a total of over 6,000 miles (9,600 km) a year. Flies north from February to May; south from late June to November. The migration route describes an oval: north along the Pacific Coast in the spring, south along the Rocky Mountains in the summer and autumn. On the southbound migration, the males leave first, then the immatures, then the females. Typically, the Rufous flies long distances, then stops to feed long enough to build up its fat reserves for another long flight. The Rufous also wanders farther afield than any other North American hummingbird: It has been spotted from Nova Scotia to Florida after the breeding season (most of these sightings are in November and December). It occasionally winters in the south in Alabama, Louisiana, Mississippi, and Texas along the Gulf Coast. Because it has a large breeding range and is inclined to roam all over the continent on its way south, its migration schedule is complicated. Just because the Rufous is not supposed to be in a certain area, don't rule it out: Vagrant is the Rufous Hummingbird's middle name.

Nesting Season: Early May to early June, peaks in May. Males arrive several weeks before the females. The male's display flight is a slanted oval, or more precisely, egg-shaped, since it is wider at the bottom. The sounds that accompany the flight make the Rufous sound like a one-man band: a loud wing buzz, followed by a high-pitched staccato whine, and finished off handsomely with a rattle. The display is repeated several times. (To distinguish the Rufous's display from the Allen's *(Selasphorus sasin)* display, note that the Rufous lacks the pendulum swing characteristic of the Allen's, and the Allen's only does his display once.) Nothing is known of coition in Rufous Hummingbirds, or how long it takes the female to build the nest, or how long she incubates the eggs.

Nests are built in a wide variety of locations, all well hidden by leaves. They have been found in alders *(Alnus spp.),* blackberry brambles *(Rubus spp.),* huckleberry bushes *(Vaccinium* spp.*),* on the drooping branches of firs *(Abies spp.),* spruce *(Picea* spp.*),* and other conifers as well as on vines and the dry roots of overturned trees. Though the Rufous renests if its first brood is destroyed, second broods are not reported. Nests are often reused in subsequent years, and some even have been found stacked three deep. The nests are 6 to 16 feet (2–5 m) above the ground. They are lined with willow down and decorated with lichens. The nestlings remain in the nest about three weeks.

Habitat: Forest edges, woodlands, meadows, foothills, canyons, chaparral, mountain ridges at timberline, seacoast, coastal islands, alpine meadows, lowland plains, and suburban gardens. Coniferous forest is the primary nesting habitat. Because of the wide range of habitats, they forage an equally wide range of flowers. They feed on agave *(Agave* spp.*),* bouvardia *(Bouvardia glaberrima),* columbine *(Aquilegia formosa,* and *A.* spp.*),* eucalypts *(Eucalyptus* spp.*),* figwort *(Scrophularia* spp.*),* fireweed *(Epilobium angustifolium),* fuchsia *(Fuchsia* spp.*),* gooseberries and currants *(Ribes sanguineum,* and *Ribes* spp.*),* honeysuckle *(Lonicera* spp.*),* Indian paintbrush *(Castilleja miniata),* larkspur *(Delphinium* spp.*),* madrone *(Arbutus menziesii),* manzanitas *(Arctostaphylos* spp.*),* ocotillo *(Fouqueria splendens),* orange blossoms *(Citrus* spp.*),* peach blossoms *(Prunus persica),* penstemon *(Penstemon* spp.*),* red-hot-poker *(Kniphofia uvaria),* Rocky Mountain bee plant *(Cleome* spp.*),* salmon berry *(Rubus spectabilis),* thimble berry *(R. parviflorus),* toad flax *(Linaria vulgaris),* and tree tobacco *(Nicotiana glauca).* They also feed on sap from sapsuckers' sap wells.

The Rufous is both the most agile and most aggressive of all hummingbird species, and where its range overlaps with the Anna's, Calliope, Broad-tailed, and Black-chinned Hummingbirds, the Rufous usually wins the battles over who gets to feed where. Threat displays to frighten off rivals include fanning the tail (both sexes) and noisy dive displays angled to make the iridescent gorget flash brilliantly (males).

Violet-crowned Hummingbird

Species: AMAZILIA VIOLICEPS (AMAZILIA VERTICALIS)

Other Names: Azure-crown, Salvin's hummingbird; Chupamirto corona azul (Spanish).

Size: 3³/₄ to 4¹/₄ inches (9.4–10.6 cm).

Field Marks:
The best field marks for both sexes are the pure white underparts and red bill with black tip. Large for a hummingbird.
MALE: Pure white underparts, red bill with black tip, green body, brilliant violet-blue crown.
FEMALE: Pure white underparts, red bill with black tip, green body, dull greenish blue crown.

Range: In the United States, found only in Guadalupe Canyon in the Peloncillo Mountains in southeastern Arizona and the adjacent corner of New Mexico where they breed. Winter range is Sonora to Chiapas, Mexico.

Migration: Nothing is known beyond the fact that the Violet-crowned Hummingbirds seen in Arizona and New Mexico are migratory. They come north in June, go south in September and October.

Nesting Season: July and August. Nothing is known of the Violet-crown's migration routes, flight displays, behavior, nesting, or breeding. Should you be fortunate enough to observe one, take careful notes, and call the local Audubon Society with the information.

Few nests have been found. Those that have are made of a white cottony material from the paloblanco tree *(Populus* spp.?, *Celtis laevigata?)* bound together with spider web, and decorated with tiny twigs and green lichens, giving the nest a green and white appearance. One nest was 1¹/₂ inches (3.8 cm) across, 1 inch (2.5 cm) deep, and the cup was ¹/₂ inch (1.25 cm) in diameter. Nests have been found in sycamores *(Platanus* spp.) and scrub oaks *(Quercus* spp.*).*

Habitat: Guadalupe Canyon has a small stream lined by cottonwoods *(Populus* spp.*),* sycamores, and other trees and bushes. Violet-crowns feed from flowering trees and agave *(Agave* spp.*).*

White-eared Hummingbird

Species: HYLOCHARIS LEUCOTIS, CYNANTHUS LEUCOTIS

Other Names: Orejas blancas, Chupaflor orejiblanco (Spanish).

Size: 3¹/₂ inches (8.75 cm).

Field Marks:
The clearest field marks for both sexes are the red bill with black tip, white ear-stripe, and black ear-patch.
MALE: Red bill with black tip, broad white stripe behind the eye, dark-green under-parts, blue-and-green throat, purple crown.
FEMALE: Red bill with black tip, white stripe behind the eye, throat spotted with irides-cent green, emerald-green back, pale gray underparts, sides speckled with metallic green, square green tail.

Range: In the United States, the White-ear is found only in the Chiricahua (Cave Creek Canyon) and Huachaca Mountains (Ramsey Canyon) of Arizona, the Animas Mountains of New Mexico, and the Chisos Mountains of Big Bend National Park, Texas. It also breeds in Mexico, Guatemala, Honduras, and Nicaragua. Winters in Mexico and Guatemala.

Migration: North in April to May; South in August to September.

Nesting Season: In the United States, June to August. They may breed year-round, depending on local conditions. In the spring, males form singing assemblies within hearing distance of each other, pick a perch, and each sings a low, clear, bell-like note incessantly. Most assemblies occur early in the morning, but the males have been heard singing from morning to night. Each assembly has its own song, slightly different from that of other assemblies, even those nearby. The primary purpose is to attract females, but it may also discourage other males from intruding on the territory. These mating stations are defended for three or four months in Guatemala. Such displays have not been observed in the United States. The female selects the male of her choice and lures him to her nesting area. She perches and he courts her, by whirring all around her. She flies to another perch, he follows, and repeats his performance. Each time she perches, she does so for a shorter time, and the flights between perches are longer. The birds make the intervening flights together, sometimes hovering face-to-face. Each time she lands, he tries to persuade her to join him in flight again. The nuptial flight is wild and darting, as they alternate looping maneuvers and hovering bill-to-bill. It ends with a final swoop as they fly off to mate.

Nests are usually in shrubs or low trees, often in *Baccaris vaccinioides,* 5 to 20 feet (1.5 to 6 m) above the ground. They also nest in oaks *(Quercus nitens, Q. reticulata).* Nests are made of the downy covering on the underside of the oak leaves, spider webbing, with green mosses and gray lichens decorating the outside. They are 2 inches

(5 cm) in diameter, the cup half as wide, and the rim is curved in. The nests range from 2 to 3 inches (2.5–7.5 cm) in height, and it takes the female fifteen to twenty days to build the nest. It takes sixty to seventy days from starting to build the nest until the young birds are fledged.

White-ears may raise two or three broods a year. Nest mortality is high: Of eighteen eggs in nine nests, only three young survived to fledging in one study, and in another study of thirty-nine nests, the nestlings of only twelve fledged.

Habitat: Pine-oak *(Pinus* spp., *Quercus* spp.*)* woods near streams, oak woodlands in mountain canyons. This species shows no preference for red flowers. They eat insects found in flowers and hawk them as well. Feeds from burmarigold *(Bidens* spp.*)*, *Cuphea jorullensis*, penstemon *(Penstemon* spp.*)*, and sage *(Salvia cinnabarina, S. cacalioefolia, S. mexicana)*.

Current ecological awareness demands that people find ways to limit human encroachment and destruction of habitat so that other species can survive on the planet. This is a particularly critical issue for hummingbirds, for the greatest numbers are found in impoverished Third World countries where clearing rain forest for farms or creating jobs logging tropical hardwoods are of more immediate importance to the local people than the preservation and protection of wildlife. These people are more concerned about their own survival than that of a species of bird they may have never seen, and that they can't eat in any case.

Costa Rica and Ecuador are two countries that have found a way to turn their wildlife wonders to good account to benefit their people. Money has flowed in from many nations to help the Monteverde Cloud Forest Preserve in Costa Rica, breeding grounds to the resplendent quetzal, as well as home to many hummingbirds. Ecuador has turned the whole of the Galápagos Islands into a wildlife refuge where all species are protected. There are no hummingbirds in the Galápagos, but mainland Ecuador has more species of hummingbird than any other country, and the tourist dollars that flow into the country from people who wish to see creatures that can't be seen anywhere except the Galápagos markedly improve Ecuador's economy. That means less wilderness land is cleared for subsistence farming, and more natural habitat is available for the hummingbirds.

Epilogue

The facts about hummingbirds are so strange, they are so unlike any other bird, or for that matter, any other living creatures, that it must have been easier for the Old World to believe in fairies and leprechauns than hummingbirds. At least leprechauns were supposed to look like little people; hummingbirds don't look like any other bird, which is probably why they were thought at one point to be part insect. They fly sideways, upside-down, and backward. They have colors that are brilliant one instant and vanish the next. They build nests fit for the most royal of fairies, lined with thistledown, woven of golden mosses, decorated with fern frond scales, the whole bound up with the silver strands of spider webs. They come out of eggs the size of peas. They are the tiniest of creatures and the most fearless. They apparently die at night and in the morning return from the dead. No, the real wonder is that all the explorers who came back with reports of such creatures were not condemned as liars or committed as madmen the moment their tales were told. Birds that hang in the air, as though suspended from a string? Impossible!

But as I write these words, there they are, Anna's Hummingbirds, hanging in the air, hovering outside my window.

Appendix

Where to Find Hummingbirds

Before scheduling a hummingbird safari, check with the local chapter of the Audubon Society for the best dates for viewing the species you want to see.

THE UNITED STATES

ARIZONA

In the summer, southeastern Arizona has the most species in North America. The best place to see the birds is the Nature Conservancy's Mile Hi Camp at the Ramsey Canyon Preserve, where as many as thirteen species have been seen, and the resident naturalists are extremely knowledgeable. The number for reservations is (602) 378-2785; the address is Mile Hi, Route 1, Box 84, Hereford, Arizona 85615. Anywhere from Tucson to Nogales east toward Portal, Douglas, Green Valley, and Madera Canyon will give you a good chance of spotting some of the rarer migratory hummingbirds. Flowering slopes of canyons with streams in the Chiricahua or Huachuca Mountains are likely to provide excellent spotting, particularly along Cave Creek. Ramsey Canyon, Sycamore Canyon, and Garden Canyon are where the researchers go, and are sufficiently well known for their hummingbirds, so that those who run local motels, campgrounds, and resorts can give you good current information on where to look.

CALIFORNIA

In southern California, the South Coast Botanical Gardens in Palos Verdes near Los Angeles at (213) 544-1847 or the Rancho Santa Ana Botanical Gardens at Claremont at (714) 625-8767 are excellent places to see hummingbirds.

LOUISIANA

Spring migrants also pass through the Hilltop Arboretum in East Baton Rouge, Louisiana.

PENNSYLVANIA

Watch the spring migration of Ruby-throated Hummingbirds at Powder Mill Nature Reserve.

TEXAS

Big Bend National Park on the Mexican border has had as many as eight species in a single day. North Padre Island is a good place to watch the spring migration.

CANADA

BRITISH COLUMBIA

Four hummingbird species can be seen during the summer in the southeastern corner of British Columbia and along the British Columbia coast: Rufous, Calliope, Anna's and Black-chinned. The Anna's has also been reported several times in the Okanagan Valley. A likely place to see hummingbirds is Butchart Gardens just outside Victoria on Vancouver Island.

ONTARIO

Watch the spring migration at Point Pelee National Park in Ontario.

THE CARIBBEAN

THE BAHAMA ISLANDS

Hummingbirds can be seen at the Freeport Botanical Gardens on Grand Bahama Island.

JAMAICA

You can have hummingbirds eating out of your hand at Lisa Salmon's Rock Bird's Feeding Station at Anchovy just outside Montego Bay in Jamaica. The telephone number is (809) 952-2009.

TRINIDAD

Hummingbirds can be observed at the Asa Wright Nature Centre in Trinidad. Contact Caligo Ventures, (800) 426-7781 in the United States, for a complete bird list and booking.

CENTRAL AMERICA

In Costa Rica a great many species can be seen at Monteverde Cloud Forest Reserve, Punta Arenas, Costa Rica, a splendid example of rare virgin cloud forest habitat. At the right time of the year, one may also see the resplendent quetzal, often called the most beautiful bird in the world. Panama also has a great many hummingbird species.

SOUTH AMERICA

The best place to see the most hummingbirds of the greatest variety of species are in South America, particularly Ecuador, Colombia, Peru, Venezuela, and Brazil. It's best to book with a birding tour or hire a knowledgeable naturalist guide.

YOUR OWN BACKYARD

At my house, a hummingbird feeder had hung for years, but it had never attracted many birds. My husband and I cleaned it thoroughly, filled it, and hung five more feeders around the house. Within a few days, the hummingbirds were eating out of our hands when we held the feeders (after first scolding us that they were not hanging in their usual places), and we have had six flying around us at once, two on the feeder in our hand, and four playing over our heads. Since Anna's Hummingbirds are resident here in Marin County, California, year-round, we are planning and planting our garden to attract more hummingbirds. The fuchsias, impatiens, petunias, pelargoniums, penstemon *(Penstemon gloxinoides),* and foxglove *(Digitalis* spp.*)* are in, the native paintbrush *(Castilleja* spp. *),* monkey flower *(Mimulus guttata),* and wild buckwheat *(Eriogonum fasciculatum)* have volunteered in the woodland garden, and the woods are full of madrones. I am committed to keeping all the feeders full, although the hummingbirds go through about four cups of nectar a day! I want the Anna's to stay here always, and the Allen's and Rufous to keep coming back year after year. I love watching the summer evening feeding frenzy with thirty-five or more hummingbirds darting and dashing every which way.

Selecting a feeder that is attractive to both people and hummingbirds can be a challenge. Smith & Hawken at (800) 776-3336 has the handsomest one I've seen; its hand-blown glass, which looks like an alchemist's flask, glows magnificently when it's filled with red nectar, and holds four cups.

A good way to attract hummingbirds is to plant your garden with nectar-rich flowers. The *Bird Watchers' Digest* identified the following species as hummingbird favorites: fuchsia (spp.), honeysuckle *(Lonicera* spp.*),* impatiens (spp.), petunia (spp.), and sages *(Salvia* spp.*).* Other excellent choices are bee balm *(Monarda* spp.*),* bleeding heart *(Dicentra* spp.*),* canna (spp.), columbine *(Aquilegia* spp.*),* coralbells *(Heuchera sanguinea* spp.*),* delphinium (spp.), foxglove *(Digitalis* spp.*),* geraniums (spp.), lilies *(Lilium* spp.*),* lupine *(Lupinus* spp.*),* nicotiana (spp.), penstemon (spp.), and phlox (spp.).

THE NORTH AMERICAN SPECIES

EASTERN AND MIDWESTERN HUMMINGBIRDS
Ruby-throated

WESTERN MOUNTAIN HUMMINGBIRDS

Black-chinned	Calliope
Broad-tailed	Rufous

WEST COAST HUMMINGBIRDS

Allen's	Calliope
Anna's	Costa's
Black-chinned	Rufous
Broad-tailed	

SOUTHWESTERN HUMMINGBIRDS

(Common)		(Uncommon)
Allen's	Broad-tailed	Berylline
Anna's	Calliope	Lucifer
Black-chinned	Costa's	Violet-crowned
Blue-throated	Magnificent	White-eared
Broad-billed		

GULF COAST HUMMINGBIRDS
Buff-bellied
Ruby-throated

Ornithological and Wildlife Conservation Organizations

American Birding Association
P.O. Box 6599
Colorado Springs, CO 80934

Canadian Nature Federation
453 Sussex Drive
Ottawa, Ontario
K1N 6Z4

National Audubon Society
950 Third Avenue
New York, NY 10022

Organization for Tropical Studies
North American Headquarters
P.O. Box DM
Duke Station
Durham, NC 27706

American Ornithologists' Union
National Museum of National History
Smithsonian Institution
Washington, DC 20560

Cooper Ornithological Society
Department of Biology
University of California
Los Angeles, CA 90024

National Wildlife Federation
1400 Sixteenth Street, N.W.
Washington, DC 20036

World Wildlife Fund
1250 24th Street, N.W.
Washington, DC 20037

Association of Field
  Ornithologists
Manomet Bird Observatory
P.O. Box 936
Manomet, MA 02345

International Council for Bird
  Preservation
United States Section
801 Pennsylvania Avenue, S.E.
Washington, DC 20003

The Nature Conservancy
79A Broadview Avenue
Toronto, Ontario
M4K 2T7

World Wildlife Fund
60 St. Clair Avenue East
Suite #201
Toronto, Ontario
M4T 1N5

Plants that Attract Hummingbirds to the Garden

Herbaceous plants:

Bee Balm	*Monarda* spp.
Begonia	*Begonia* spp.
Blazing Star	*Liatris* spp.
Bleeding Heart	*Dicentra* spp.
Butterfly-Weed	*Asclepias tuberosa*
Canna	*Canna generalis*
Cardinal Flower	*Lobelia cardinalis*
Carpet Bugle	*Ajuga reptans*
Century Plant	*Agave americana*
Columbine	*Aquilegia* spp.
Coral-Bells	*Heuchera sanguinea*
Dahlia	*Dahlia merckii*
Dame's Rocket	*Hesperis matronalis*
Delphinium	*Delphinium* spp.
Fire Pink	*Silene virginica*
Flowering Tobacco	*Nicotiana alata*
Four-o'Clock	*Mirabilis jalapa*
Foxglove	*Digitalis* spp.
Fuchsia	*Fuchsia* spp.
Gilia	*Gilia* spp.
Geranium	*Pelargonium* spp.
Gladiolus	*Gladiolus* spp.
Hollyhock	*Althea* spp.
Impatiens	*Impatiens* spp.
Lantana	*Lantana camara*
Lily	*Lilium* spp.
Lupine	*Lupinus* spp.
Nasturtium	*Tropaeolum majus*
Paintbrush	*Castilleja* spp.
Penstemon	*Penstemon* spp.
Petunia	*Petunia* spp.
Phlox	*Phlox* spp.
Red-Hot Poker	*Kniphofia uvaria*
Scabiosa	*Scabiosa* spp.
Scarlet Sage	*Salvia splendens*
Spider Flower	*Cleome spinosa*
Sweet William	*Dianthus barbatus*
Verbena	*Verbena* spp.
Yucca	*Yucca* spp.
Zinnia	*Zinnia* spp.

Shrubs:

Abelia	*Abelia grandiflora*
Azalea	*Rhododendron* spp.
Bearberry	*Arctostaphylos* spp.
Beauty Bush	*Kolkwitzia amabilis*
Beloperone	*Beloperone californica*
Butterfly Bush	*Buddleia Davidii*
Cape Honeysuckle	*Tecomaria capensis*
Currant	*Ribes odoratum*
Flowering Quince	*Chaenomeles japonica*
Gooseberry	*Ribes speciosum*
Hardy Fuchsia	*Fuchcia magellanica*
Hibiscus	*Hibiscus* spp.
Honeysuckle	*Lonicera* spp.
Jasmine	*Jasminum* spp.
Scarlet Bush	*Hamelia erecta*

Weigela	*Weigela* spp.

Vines:

Cypress-Vine	*Quamoclit* spp.
Honeysuckle	*Lonicera Heckrottii*
Morning Glory	*Ipomea* spp.
Scarlet Runner-Bean	*Phaseolus coccineus*
Trumpet Creeper	*Campsis radicans*
Trumpet Honeysuckle	*Lonicera sempervirens*

Trees:

Chaste-Tree	*Vitem agnus-castus*
Chinaberry	*Melia azedarach*
Cockspur Coralbean	*Erythrina cristi-galli*
Eucalyptus	*Eucalyptus* spp.
Flowering Crab	*Malus* spp.
Hawthorn	*Crataegus* spp.
Horse Chestnut	*Aesculus glabra*
Locust	*Robinia* spp.
Orange Tree	*Citrus* spp.
Palo Verde	*Cercidium microphyllum*
Poinciana	*Caesalpinia* spp.
Red Buckeye	*Aesculus carnea*
Royal Poinciana	*Delonix regia*
Siberian Pea Tree	*Caragana arborescens*
Silk Oak	*Grevillea robusta*
Silk Tree	*Albizia Julibrissin*
Tree Tobacco	*Nicotiana glauca*
Tulip Poplar	*Liriodendron tulipifera*

Wildflower, Native Plant, and Gardening Organizations

American Association of Botanical
 Gardens and Arboreta
P.O. Box 206
Swarthmore, PA 19081

American Forestry Association
P.O. Box 2000
Washington, DC 20013

American Horticultural Society
P.O. Box 0105
Mount Vernon, VA 22121

Canadian Plant Conservation
 Program
c/o Devonian Botanic Garden
University of Alberta
Edmonton, Alberta
T6G 2E1

Canadian Wildflower Society
1848 Liverpool Road
Box 110
Pickering, Ontario L1V 6M3

Civic Garden Centre
777 Lawrence Avenue East
(in Edwards Gardens)
Toronto, Ontario
M3C 1P2

The Garden Club of America
598 Madison Avenue
New York, NY
10022

National Gardening Association
180 Flynn Avenue
Burlington, VT
05401

National Wildflower Research
 Center
2600 FM 973 North
Austin, TX 78725

Hummingbird Species of the World

Common Name	*Latin Name*	*Range*
Allen's Hummingbird	*Selasphorus (Selasphorus) sasin*	USA and Mexico
Amazilia Hummingbird	*Amazilia (Amazilia) amazilia*	Ecuador and Peru
Amethyst Woodstar	*Calliphlox (Calothorax) amethystina*	Bolivia to Argentina
Amethyst-throated Hummingbird	*Lampornis amethystinus*	Mexico to Honduras
Amethyst-throated Sunangel	*Heliangelus amethysticollis*	Venezuela to Bolivia
Andean Emerald	*Amazilia (Polyerata) franciae*	Colombia to Peru
Andean Hillstar	*Oreotrochilus estella*	Ecuador to Argentina, Chile
Anna's Hummingbird	*Archilochus (Calypte) anna*	USA and Mexico
Antillean Crested Hummingbird	*Orthorhyncus cristatus*	Lesser Antilles
Antillean Mango	*Anthracothorax dominicus*	West Indies
Bahama Woodstar	*Calothorax (Philodice) evelynae*	Bahamas
Band-tailed Barbthroat	*Threnetes (Glaucis) ruckeri*	Guatemala to Ecuador
Bearded Coquette	*Lophornis (Lophornis) insignibarbis*	Unknown
Bearded Helmetcrest	*Oxypogon guerinii*	Venezuela and Colombia
Bearded Mountaineer	*Oreonympha nobilis*	Peru
Beautiful Hummingbird	*Calothorax (Calothorax) pulcher*	Mexico
Bee Hummingbird	*Archilochus (Calypte) helenae*	Cuba
Berlepsch Emerald	*Chlorostilbon inexpectatus*	Colombia
Berlioz Woodnymph	*Augasmall (Cyanophaia) cyaneoberyllina*	Brazil (Bahia)
Berylline Hummingbird	*Amazilia (Saucerottia) beryllina*	Mexico to Honduras
Black Barbthroat	*Threnetes (Glaucis) grzimeki*	Brazil (Southeast)
Black Inca	*Coeligena prunellei*	Colombia
Black Jacobin	*Melanotrochilus (Florisuga) fuscus*	Brazil (East and Central)
Black Metaltail	*Metallura phoebe*	Peru and Bolivia
Black-backed Thornbill	*Ramphomicron (Chalcostigma) dorsale*	Colombia
Black-bellied Hummingbird	*Eupherusa (Chalybura) nigriventris*	Costa Rica and Panama
Black-bellied Thorntail	*Lophornis (Popelairia) langsdorffi*	Venezuela to Brazil, Peru
Black-billed Hermit	*Phaethornis nigirostris*	Brazil (Southeast)
Black-breasted Hillstar	*Oreotrochilus melanogaster*	Peru
Black-breasted Plovercrest	*Stephanoxis lalandi*	Brazil to Argentina
Black-breasted Puffleg	*Eriocnemis nigrivestis*	Ecuador
Black-chinned Hummingbird	*Archilochus (Archilochus) alexandri*	Canada to Mexico

Common Name	Latin Name	Range
Black-crested Coquette	*Lophornis (Lophornis) helenae*	Mexico to Costa Rica
Black-eared Fairy	*Heliothryx aurita*	Guianas to Bolivia, Brazil
Black-fronted Hummingbird	*Cynanthus (Basilinna) xantusii*	Mexico (Baja California)
Black-hooded Sunbeam	*Aglaeactis pamela*	Bolivia
Black-tailed Trainbearer	*Lesbia victoriae*	Colombia to Peru
Black-thighed Puffleg	*Eriocnemis derbyi*	Colombia and Ecuador
Black-throated Brilliant	*Heliodoxa (Heliodoxa) schreibersii*	Ecuador to Peru
Black-throated Mango	*Anthracothorax nigricollis*	Panama to Argentina
Blossomcrown	*Anthocephala floriceps*	Colombia
Blue-capped (Oaxaca) Hummingbird	*Eupherusa (Chalybura) cyanophrys*	Mexico
Blue-capped Puffleg	*Eriocnemis glaucopoides*	Bolivia to Argentina
Blue-chested Hummingbird	*Amazilia (Polyerata) amabilis*	Nicaragua to Ecuador
Blue-chinned Sapphire	*Chlorestes (Chorostilbon) notatus*	Guianas to Peru
Blue-fronted Lancebill	*Doryfera johannae*	Guyana to Peru
Blue-headed Hummingbird	*Cyanophaia bicolor*	Lesser Antilles
Blue-headed Sapphire	*Cynanthus (Eucephala) grayi*	Panama to Ecuador
Blue-mantled Thornbill	*Chalcostigma stanleyi*	Ecuador and Bolivia
Blue-spotted Hummingbird	*Amazilia (Polyerata) cyaneotincta*	Unknown
Blue-tailed Emerald	*Chlorostilbon mellisugus*	Costa Rica to Brazil
Blue-tailed Hummingbird	*Amazilia (Saucerottia) cyanura*	Mexico to Costa Rica
Blue-throated Goldentail	*Cynanthus (Hylocharis) eliciae*	Mexico to Panama
Blue-throated Hummingbird	*Lampornis clemenciae*	USA to Mexico
Blue-throated Starfrontlet	*Coeligena helianthea*	Venezuela and Colombia
Blue-tufted Starthroat	*Heliomaster furcifer*	Colombia to Argentina
Booted Racket-tail	*Ocreatus underwoodii*	Venezuela to Bolivia
Brazilian Ruby	*Clytolaema rubricauda*	Brazil (Southeast)
Broad-billed Hummingbird	*Cynanthus (Cynanthus) latirostris*	USA and Mexico
Broad-tailed Hummingbird	*Selasphorus (Selasphorus) platycercus*	USA to Guatemala
Broad-tipped Hermit	*Phaethornis gounellei*	Brazil (Northeast)
Bronze-tailed Barbthroat	*Threnetes (Glaucis) loehkeni*	Brazil (Amapá)
Bronze-tailed Comet	*Polyonymus (Lesbia) caroli*	Peru
Bronze-tailed Plumeleteer	*Chalybura urochrysia*	Nicaragua to Ecuador
Bronze-tailed Thornbill	*Chalcostigma heteropogon*	Venezuela and Colombia
Bronzy Hermit	*Glaucis aenea*	Nicaragua to Ecuador
Bronzy Inca	*Coeligena coeligena*	Venezuela to Bolivia

Common Name	*Latin Name*	*Range*
Brown Inca	*Coeligena wilsoni*	Colombia and Ecuador
Brown Violet-ear	*Colibri delphinae*	Mexico to Brazil
Buff-bellied Hermit	*Phaethornis subochraceus*	Bolivia and Brazil
Buff-bellied Hummingbird	*Amazilia (Amazilia) yucatanensis*	USA to Honduras
Buff-breasted Sabrewing	*Campylopterus duidae*	Venezuela and Brazil
Buff-tailed Coronet	*Boissonneaua flavescens*	Venezuela to Ecuador
Buff-tailed Sicklebill	*Eutoxeres condamini*	Colombia to Peru
Buff-winged Starfrontlet	*Coeligena lutetiae*	Colombia and Ecuador
Buffy Hummingbird	*Leucippus fallax*	Colombia and Venezuela
Bumblebee Hummingbird	*Selasphorus (Atthis) heloisa*	Mexico
Cabanis Emerald	*Chlorostilbon auratus*	Peru
Calliope Hummingbird	*Archilochus (Stellula) calliope*	Canada to Mexico
Cerise-throated Hummingbird	*Selasphorus (Selasphorus) simoni*	Costa Rica
Chestnut-bellied Hummingbird	*Amazilia (Amazilia) castaneiventris*	Colombia
Chestnut-breasted Coronet	*Boissonneaua matthewsii*	Colombia to Peru
Chilean Woodstar	*Eulidia (Myrtis) yarrellii*	Chile
Christina Barbthroat	*Threnetes (Glaucis) cristinae*	Brazil (Amapá)
Cinnamon Hummingbird	*Amazilia (Amazilia) rutila*	Mexico to Costa Rica
Cinnamon-throated Hermit	*Phaethornis nattereri*	Brazil and Bolivia
Collared Inca	*Coeligena torquata*	Venezuela to Bolivia
Colorful Puffleg	*Eriocnemis mirabilis*	Colombia
Copper-rumped Hummingbird	*Amazilia (Saucerottia) tobaci*	Venezuela, Trinidad, Tobago
Coppery Emerald	*Chlorostilbon russatus*	Venezuela and Colombia
Coppery Metaltail	*Metallura theresiae*	Peru
Coppery Thorntail	*Lophornis (Popelairia) letitiae*	Bolivia
Coppery-bellied Puffleg	*Eriocnemis cupreoventris*	Venezuela and Colombia
Coppery-headed Emerald	*Elvira (Chalybura) cupreiceps*	Costa Rica
Costa's Hummingbird	*Archilochus (Calypte) costae*	USA and Mexico
Crimson Topaz	*Topaza pella*	Guianas to Ecuador
Crowned (Fork-tailed) Woodnymph	*Thalurania (Cyanophaia) furcata*	Mexico to Ecuador, Argentina
Cuban Emerald	*Chlorostilbon ricordii*	Cuba and Bahamas
Decorated Woodstar	*Acestrura decorata*	Colombia
Dot-eared Coquette	*Lophornis (Lophornis) gouldii*	Brazil (North and Central)
Dusky Coquette	*Lophornis (Lophornis) melaniae*	Colombia
Dusky Hummingbird	*Cynanthus (Cynanthus) sordidus*	Mexico

Common Name	Latin Name	Range
Dusky Starfrontlet	*Coeligena orina*	Colombia
Dusky-throated Hermit	*Phaethornis squalidus*	Colombia to Brazil
Ecuadorean Piedtail	*Phlogophilus hemileucurus*	Ecuador
Emerald Woodnymph	*Augasmall (Cyanophaia) smaragdinea*	Brazil (Southeast)
Emerald-bellied Puffleg	*Eriocnemis alinae*	Colombia to Peru
Emerald-chinned Hummingbird	*Abeillia abeillei*	Mexico to Nicaragua
Empress Brilliant	*Heliodoxa (Heliodoxa) imperatrix*	Colombia and Ecuador
Escudo Hummingbird	*Amazilia (Amazilia) handleyi*	Panama
Esmeralda Woodstar	*Acestrura berlepschi*	Ecuador
Fawn-breasted Brilliant	*Heliodoxa (Heliodoxa) rubinoides*	Colombia to Peru
Festive Coquette	*Lophornis (Lophornis) chalybea*	Venezuela to Brazil
Fiery Topaz	*Topaza pyra*	Venezuela to Peru
Fiery-tailed Awlbill	*Avocettula (Sericotes) recurvirostris*	Guianas to Ecuador
Fiery-throated Hummingbird	*Panterpe (Lampornis) insignis*	Costa Rica and Panama
Fire-throated Metaltail	*Metallura eupogon*	Peru and Bolivia
Flame-rumped Sapphire	*Cynanthus (Hylocharis) pyropygia*	Brazil (Bahia)
Fork-tailed Emerald	*Chlorostilbon canivetti*	Mexico to Venezuela
Frilled Coquette	*Lophornis (Lophornis) magnifica*	Brazil (East and Central)
Garnet-throated Hummingbird	*Lamprolaima (Lampornis) rhami*	Mexico to Honduras
Giant Hummingbird	*Patagona gigas*	Ecuador to Chile
Gilded Hummingbird	*Cynanthus (Hylocharis) chrysura*	Brazil to Argentina
Glistening Sunangel	*Heliangelus luminosus*	Unknown
Glittering Emerald	*Chlorostilbon aureoventris*	Brazil to Argentina
Glittering-throated Emerald	*Amazilia (Polyerata) fimbriata*	Guianas to Bolivia
Glow-throated Hummingbird	*Selasphorus (Selasphorus) ardens*	Panama
Glowing Puffleg	*Eriocnemis vestitus*	Venezuela to Ecuador
Golden-bellied Starfrontlet	*Coeligena bonapartei*	Venezuela and Colombia
Golden-breasted Puffleg	*Eriocnemis mosquera*	Colombia and Ecuador
Golden-tailed Sapphire	*Chrysuronia (Cynanthus) oenone*	Venezuela to Brazil
Gorgeted Sunangel	*Heliangelus strophianus*	Colombia and Ecuador
Gorgeted Woodstar	*Acestrura heliodor*	Panama to Ecuador
Gould Jewelfront	*Polyplancta (Clytolaema) aurescens*	Venezuela to Brazil
Gray-bellied Comet	*Taphrolesbia griseiventris*	Peru
Gray-breasted Sabrewing	*Campylopterus largipennis*	Guianas to Brazil
Gray-chinned Hermit	*Phaethornis griseogularis*	Venezuela to Peru

Common Name	Latin Name	Range
Great Sapphirewing	Pterophanes cyanopterus	Colombia to Bolivia
Great-billed Hermit	Phaethornis malaris	Cayenne to Brazil
Green Hermit	Phaethornis guy	Costa Rica to Peru
Green Mango	Anthracothorax viridis	Puerto Rico
Green Thorntail	Lophornis (Popelairia) conversii	Costa Rica to Ecuador
Green Violet-ear	Colibri thalassinus	Mexico to Bolivia
Green-and-white Hummingbird	Amazilia (Leucippus) viridicauda	Peru
Green-backed Firecrown	Sephanoides sephanoides	Argentina and Chile
Green-bellied Hummingbird	Amazilia (Saucerottia) viridigaster	Guyana to Colombia
Green-breasted Mango	Anthracothorax prevostii	Mexico to Peru
Green-crowned Brilliant	Heliodoxa (Heliodoxa) jacula	Costa Rica to Ecuador
Green-fronted Hummingbird	Amazilia (Amazilia) viridifrons	Mexico
Green-fronted Lancebill	Doryfera ludovicae	Costa Rica to Bolivia
Green-tailed Emerald	Chlorostilbon alice	Venezuela
Green-tailed Goldenthroat	Polytmus theresiae	Guianas to Brazil
Green-tailed Trainbearer	Lesbia nuna	Venezuela to Bolivia
Green-throated Carib	Sericotes holosericeus	West Indies
Green-throated Mango	Anthracothorax viridigula	Venezuela to Brazil
Green-throated Mountain-gem	Lampornis viridipallens	Mexico to Honduras
Green-throated Sunangel	Heliangelus speciosa	Unknown
Greenish Puffleg	Haplophaedia (Eriocnemis) aureliae	Panama to Bolivia
Hartert Woodstar	Acestrura harterti	Colombia
Heliotrope-throated Hummingbird	Selasphorus (Selasphorus) torridus	Costa Rica and Panama
Hispaniolan Emerald	Chlorostilbon swainsonii	Hispaniola
Hoary Puffleg	Haplophaedia (Eriocnemis) lugens	Colombia and Ecuador
Honduras Emerald	Amazilia (Polyerata) luciae	Honduras
Hooded Visorbearer	Augastes lumachellus	Brazil (East)
Hook-billed Hermit	Glaucis dohrnii	Brazil (Southeast)
Horned Sungem	Heliactin cornuta	Surinam to Brazil
Hyacinth Visorbearer	Augastes scutatus	Brazil (East)
Indigo-capped Hummingbird	Amazilia (Saucerottia) cyanifrons	Costa Rica, Colombia
Isaacson Puffleg	Eriocnemis isaacsonii	Unknown
Jamaican Mango	Anthracothorax mango	Jamaica
Juan Fernandez Firecrown	Sephanoides fernandensis	Juan Fernandez Island
Koepcke Hermit	Phaethornis koepckeae	Peru

Common Name	Latin Name	Range
Lazuline Sabrewing	Campylopterus falcatus	Venezuela to Ecuador
Lerch Woodnymph	Thalurania (Cyanophaia) lerchi	Unknown
Little Hermit	Phaethornis longuemareus	Mexico to Brazil
Little Sunangel	Heliangelus micrastur	Ecuador to Peru
Little Woodstar	Acestrura bombus	Ecuador and Peru
Long-billed Starthroat	Heliomaster longirostris	Mexico to Bolivia
Long-tailed Hermit	Phaethornis superciliosus	Mexico to Brazil
Long-tailed Sylph	Aglaiocercus kingi	Venezuela to Bolivia
Long-tailed Woodnymph	Thalurania (Cyanophaia) watertonii	Brazil (Coastal)
Lucifer Hummingbird	Calothorax (Calothorax) lucifer	USA to Mexico
Magenta-throated Woodstar	Calothorax (Philodice) bryantae	Costa Rica and Panama
Mangrove Hummingbird	Amazilia (Polyerata) boucardi	Costa Rica
Many-spotted Hummingbird	Taphrospilus (Leucippus) hypostictus	Ecuador to Argentina
Maranhão Hermit	Phaethornis maranhaoensis	Brazil (Imperatriz)
Margaretta Hermit	Phaethornis margarettae	Brazil (Southeast)
Marvellous Spatuletail	Loddigesia mirabilis	Peru
Merida Sunangel	Heliangelus spencei	Venezuela
Mexican Sheartail	Calothorax (Doricha) eliza	Mexico
Minute Hermit	Phaethornis idaliae	Brazil (Southeast)
Mountain Avocetbill	Opisthoprora euryptera	Colombia and Ecuador
Mountain Velvetbreast	Lafresnaya lafresnayi	Venezuela to Peru
Napo Sabrewing	Campylopterus villaviscensio	Ecuador
Narrow-tailed Emerald	Chlorostilbon stenura	Venezuela and Colombia
Natterer Emerald	Chlorostilbon iolaima	Brazil (Ypanema)
Neblina Metaltail	Metallura odomae	Peru
Needle-billed Hermit	Phaethornis philippii	Peru and Brazil
Nerkhorn Hummingbird	Neolesbia nehrkorni	Unknown
Oasis Hummingbird	Rhodopsis vesper	Peru to Chile
Olivaceous Thornbill	Chalcostigma olivaceum	Peru and Bolivia
Olive-spotted Hummingbird	Leucippus chlorocercus	Ecuador to Brazil
Orange-throated Sunangel	Heliangelus mavors	Venezuela and Colombia
Pale-bellied Hermit	Phaethornis anthophilus	Panama to Venezuela
Pale-tailed Barbthroat	Threnetes (Glaucis) leucurus	Guianas to Bolivia
Peacock Coquette	Lophornis (Lophornis) pavonina	Guyana and Venezuela
Perija Metaltail	Metallura iracunda	Colombia and Venezuela

Common Name	Latin Name	Range
Peruvian Piedtail	*Phlogophilus harterti*	Peru
Peruvian Sheartail	*Thaumastura cora*	Peru
Pink-throated Brilliant	*Heliodoxa (Heliodoxa) gularis*	Colombia to Ecuador
Pirre Hummingbird	*Goethalsia (Goldmania) bella*	Panama and Colombia
Plain-bellied Emerald	*Amazilia (Polyerata) leucogaster*	Venezuela to Brazil
Plain-capped Starthroat	*Heliomaster constantii*	Mexico to Costa Rica
Planalto Hermit	*Phaethornis pretrei*	Brazil to Argentina
Puerto Rican Emerald	*Chlorostilbon maugaeus*	Puerto Rico
Purple-backed Sunbeam	*Aglaeactis aliciae*	Peru
Purple-backed Thornbill	*Ramphomicron (Chalcostigma) microrhynchum*	Venezuela to Peru
Purple-chested Hummingbird	*Amazilia (Polyerata) rosenbergi*	Colombia and Ecuador
Purple-collared Woodstar	*Myrtis fanny*	Ecuador and Peru
Purple-crowned Fairy	*Heliothryx barroti*	Mexico to Ecuador
Purple-tailed Comet	*Zodalia (Lesbia?) glyceria*	Colombia and Ecuador
Purple-tailed Thornbill	*Ramphomicron (Chalcostigma) purpureicauda*	Ecuador
Purple-throated Carib	*Eulampis (Sericotes) jugularis*	Lesser Antilles
Purple-throated Mountain-gem	*Lampornis calolaema*	Costa Rica to Panama
Purple-throated Sunangel	*Heliangelus viola*	Ecuador to Peru
Purple-throated Woodstar	*Calothorax (Philodice) mitchellii*	Colombia and Ecuador
Racket-tailed Coquette	*Lophornis (Discosura) longicauda*	Guianas to Brazil, Venezuela
Rainbow Starfrontlet	*Coeligena iris*	Ecuador and Peru
Rainbow-bearded Thornbill	*Chalcostigma herrani*	Colombia and Ecuador
Red-billed Azurecrown	*Amazilia (Polyerata) cyanocephala*	Mexico to Nicaragua
Red-billed Emerald	*Chlorostilbon gibsoni*	Venezuela and Colombia
Red-tailed Comet	*Sappho (Lesbia) sparganura*	Bolivia to Argentina
Reddish Hermit	*Phaethornis ruber*	Guianas to Bolivia
Rivoli (Magnificent) Hummingbird	*Heliodoxa (Eugenes) fulgens*	USA to Panama
Rothschild Sunangel	*Heliangelus rothschildi*	Unknown
Royal Sunangel	*Heliangelus regalis*	Peru
Ruby-throated Hummingbird	*Archilochus (Archilochus) colubris*	USA and Canada to Panama (Winter)
Ruby-topaz Hummingbird	*Orthorhyncus mosquitus*	Guianas to Bolivia, Brazil
Rufous Hummingbird	*Selasphorus (Selasphorus) rufus*	Alaska to Mexico
Rufous Sabrewing	*Campylopterus rufus*	Mexico to El Salvador
Rufous-breasted Hermit	*Glaucis hirsuta*	Panama to Brazil
Rufous-breasted Sabrewing	*Campylopterus hyperythrus*	Venezuela and Brazil

Common Name	Latin Name	Range
Rufous-capped Thornbill	*Chalcostigma ruficeps*	Ecuador and Bolivia
Rufous-crested Coquette	*Lophornis (Lophornis) delattrei*	Mexico to Bolivia
Rufous-shafted Woodstar	*Chaetocercus (Acestrura) jourdanii*	Venezuela, Colombia, Trinidad
Rufous-tailed Hummingbird	*Amazilia (Amazilia) tzacatl*	Mexico to Ecuador
Rufous-throated Sapphire	*Cynanthus (Hylocharis) sapphirina*	Peru to Argentina
Rufous-webbed Brilliant	*Heliodoxa (Heliodoxa) branickii*	Peru and Bolivia
Santa Marta Sabrewing	*Campylopterus phainopeplus*	Colombia
Sapphire-bellied Hummingbird	*Lepidopyga (Cynanthus) lilliae*	Colombia
Sapphire-spangled Emerald	*Amazilia (Polyerata) lactea*	Venezuela to Brazil
Sapphire-throated Hummingbird	*Lepidopyga (Cynanthus) coeruleogularis*	Panama and Colombia
Sapphire-vented Puffleg	*Eriocnemis luciani*	Colombia to Peru
Saw-billed Hermit	*Ramphodon (Androdon) naevius*	Brazil (Southeast)
Scale-throated Hermit	*Phaethornis eurynome*	Brazil to Argentina
Scaled Metaltail	*Metallura aeneocauda*	Venezuela to Bolivia
Scaly-breasted Hummingbird	*Phaeochroa (Aphantochroa) cuvierii*	Guatemala to Colombia
Scintillant Hummingbird	*Selasphorus (Selasphorus) scintilla*	Costa Rica and Panama
Scissor-tailed Hummingbird	*Hylonympha (Heliodoxa) macrocerca*	Venezuela
Shining Sunbeam	*Aglaeactis cupripennis*	Colombia to Peru
Shining-green Hummingbird	*Lepidopyga (Cynanthus) goudoti*	Venezuela and Colombia
Short-tailed Emerald	*Chlorostilbon poortmani*	Venezuela and Colombia
Short-tailed Woodstar	*Myrmia (Acestrura) micrura*	Ecuador and Peru
Slender Sheartail	*Calothorax (Doricha) enicura*	Mexico to Honduras
Slender-tailed Woodstar	*Microstilbon burmeisteri*	Bolivia to Argentina
Small-billed Azurecrown	*Amazilia (Polyerata) microrhyncha*	Honduras?
Snowcap	*Microchera albocoronata*	Honduras to Panama
Snowy-breasted Hummingbird	*Amazilia (Saucerottia) edward*	Panama and Costa Rica
Söderström Puffleg	*Eriocnemis soderstromi*	Ecuador
Sombre Hummingbird	*Aphantochroa cirrochloris*	Brazil (East)
Sooty Barbthroat	*Threnetes (Glaucis) niger*	Cayenne, Brazil (Amapá)
Sooty-capped Hermit	*Phaethornis augusti*	Guyana to Colombia
Spangled Coquette	*Lophornis (Lophornis) strictolopha*	Venezuela to Peru
Sparkling Violet-ear	*Colibri coruscans*	Venezuela to Argentina
Sparkling-tailed (Dupont) Hummingbird	*Tilmatura (Calothorax) dupontii*	Mexico to Nicaragua
Speckled Hummingbird	*Adelomyia melanogenys*	Venezuela to Argentina

Common Name	Latin Name	Range
Spot-throated Hummingbird	*Leucippus taczanowskii*	Peru
Steely-vented Hummingbird	*Amazilia (Saucerottia) saucerottei*	Nicaragua to Venezuela
Straight-billed Hermit	*Phaethornis bourcieri*	Guianas to Peru, Brazil
Streamertail	*Trochilus polytmus*	Jamaica
Stripe-breasted Starthroat	*Heliomaster squamosus*	Brazil (East)
Stripe-tailed Hummingbird	*Eupherusa (Chalybura) eximia*	Mexico to Panama
Swallow-tailed Hummingbird	*Eupetomena (Campylopterus) macroura*	Mexico to Paraguay
Sword-billed Hummingbird	*Ensifera ensifera*	Venezuela to Bolivia
Tachira Emerald	*Amazilia (Polyerata) distans*	Venezuela
Tawny-bellied Hermit	*Phaethornis syrmatophorus*	Colombia to Peru
Tepui Goldenthroat	*Polytmus milleri*	Venezuela
Tooth-billed Hummingbird	*Androdon aequatorialis*	Panama to Ecuador
Tourmaline Sunangel	*Heliangelus exortis*	Colombia and Peru
Tufted Coquette	*Lophornis (Lophornis) ornata*	Guianas to Brazil, Trinidad
Tumbes Hummingbird	*Leucippus baeri*	Peru
Turquoise-throated Puffleg	*Eriocnemis godini*	Ecuador, Colombia?
Tyrian Metaltail	*Metallura tyrianthina*	Ecuador, Venezuela, Bolivia
Velvet-browed Brilliant	*Heliodoxa (Heliodoxa) xanthogonys*	Guyana to Brazil
Velvet-purple Coronet	*Boissonneaua jardini*	Colombia and Ecuador
Veraguan Mango	*Anthracothorax veraguensis*	Panama
Veridian Metaltail	*Metallura williami*	Colombia and Ecuador
Versicolored Emerald	*Amazilia (Polyerata) versicolor*	Venezuela to Argentina
Vervain Hummingbird	*Archilochus (Mellisuga) minima*	West Indies
Violet Sabrewing	*Campylopterus hemileucurus*	Mexico to Panama
Violet-bellied Hummingbird	*Damophila (Cynanthus) julie*	Panama to Ecuador
Violet-capped Hummingbird	*Goldmania violiceps*	Panama and Colombia
Violet-capped Woodnymph	*Thalurania (Cyanophaia) glaucopis*	Brazil to Argentina
Violet-chested Hummingbird	*Sternoclyta cyanopectus*	Venezuela
Violet-crowned Hummingbird	*Amazilia (Amazilia) violiceps*	USA to Mexico
Violet-fronted Brilliant	*Heliodoxa (Heliodoxa) leadbeateri*	Venezuela to Bolivia
Violet-headed Hummingbird	*Klais (Abeillia) guimeti*	Honduras to Bolivia
Violet-tailed Sylph	*Aglaiocercus coelestis*	Colombia and Ecuador
Violet-throated Metaltail	*Metallura baroni*	Ecuador
Violet-throated Starfrontlet	*Coeligena violifer*	Peru and Bolivia
Volcano (Rose-throated) Hummingbird	*Selasphorus (Selasphorus) flammula*	Costa Rica

Common Name	Latin Name	Range
Wedge-billed Hummingbird	Augastes (Schistes) geoffroyi	Venezuela to Bolivia
Wedge-tailed Hillstar	Oreotrochilus adela	Bolivia
Wedge-tailed Sabrewing	Campylopterus curvipennis	Mexico to Guatemala
White-bearded Hermit	Phaethornis hispidus	Venezuela to Brazil
White-bellied Emerald	Amazilia (Polyerata) candida	Mexico to Costa Rica
White-bellied Hummingbird	Amazilia (Leucippus) chionogaster	Peru to Argentina
White-bellied Mountain-gem	Lampornis hemileucus	Costa Rica and Panama
White-bellied Woodstar	Acestrura mulsant	Colombia to Bolivia
White-browed Hermit	Phaethornis stuarti	Peru and Bolivia
White-chested Emerald	Amazilia (Polyerata) chionopectus	Guianas and Venezuela
White-chinned Sapphire	Cynanthus (Hylocharis) cyanus	Peru to Brazil
White-crested Coquette	Lophornis (Lophornis) adorabilis	Costa Rica and Panama
White-eared Hummingbird	Cynanthus (Basilinna) leucotis	USA to Nicaragua
White-necked Jacobin	Florisuga mellivora	Mexico to Brazil
White-sided Hillstar	Oreotrochilus leucopleurus	Bolivia to Argentina, Chile
White-tailed Emerald	Elvira (Chalybura) chionura	Costa Rica and Panama
White-tailed Goldenthroat	Polytmus guainumbi	Guianas to Argentina
White-tailed Hillstar	Urochroa bougueri	Colombia and Ecuador
White-tailed Hummingbird	Eupherusa (Chalybura) poliocerca	Mexico
White-tailed Sabrewing	Campylopterus ensipennis	Venezuela, Trinidad, Tobago
White-tailed Starfrontlet	Coeligena phalerata	Colombia
White-throated Hummingbird	Leucochloris albicollis	Brazil to Argentina
White-throated (Variable) Mountain-gem	Lampornis castaneoventris	Costa Rica and Panama
White-tipped Sicklebill	Eutoxeres aquila	Costa Rica to Peru
White-tufted Sunbeam	Aglaeactis castelnaudii	Peru
White-vented Plumeleteer	Chalybura buffonii	Panama to Ecuador
White-vented Violet-ear	Colibri serrirostris	Bolivia to Argentina
White-whiskered Hermit	Phaethornis yaruqui	Colombia to Ecuador
Whitetip	Urosticte benjamini	Colombia to Peru
Wine-throated Hummingbird	Selasphorus (Atthis) ellioti	Mexico to Honduras
Wire-crested Thorntail	Lophornis (Popelairia) popelairii	Colombia to Peru

Bibliography

Bent, A.C. *Life Histories of North American Cuckoos, Goatsuckers, Hummingbirds, and their Allies.* New York: Dover Publications, 1964.

Bond, James. *Birds of the West Indies, 2d ed.* Boston: Houghton Mifflin, 1971.

de Schauensee, R.M. and W.H. Phelps. *A Guide to the Birds of Venezuela.* Princeton, NJ: Princeton University Press, 1978.

Greenewalt, Crawford H. *Hummingbirds.* Garden City, New York: Doubleday & Co. and The Museum of Natural History, 1960.

Holmgren, Virginia C. *The Way of the Hummingbird.* Santa Barbara, CA: Capra Press, 1986.

Johnsgard, Paul A. *The Hummingbirds of North America.* Washington, DC: Smithsonian Institution Press, 1983.

Peters, J.L. *Check-list of Birds of the World,* Vol. 5. Cambridge, MA: Harvard University Press, 1945.

Peterson, Roger Tory, and E.L. Chalif. *A Field Guide to Mexican Birds.* Boston: Houghton Mifflin, 1973.

—————————. *A Field Guide to the Birds.* Boston: Houghton Mifflin, 1980.

—————————. *A Field Guide to Western Birds,* 3d ed. Boston: Houghton Mifflin, 1990.

Ridgeley, R.S. *A Guide to the Birds of Panama.* Princeton, NJ: Princeton University Press, 1981.

Scheithauer, Walter. *Hummingbirds.* New York: Thomas Y. Crowell Company, 1967.

Skutch, Alexander. *The Life of the Hummingbird.* New York: Crown Publishers, 1973.

Stiles, Gary, and Alexander Skutch. *A Guide to the Birds of Costa Rica.* Ithaca, NY: Cornell University Press, 1989.

Stokes, Lillian and Donald. *The Hummingbird Book: The Complete Guide to Attracting, Identifying, and Enjoying Hummingbirds.* Boston: Little, Brown and Company, 1989.

Tekulsky, Mathew. *The Hummingbird Garden.* New York: Crown Publishers, 1990.

Tyrrell, Esther Quesada and Robert A. *Hummingbirds: Their Life and Behavior.* New York: Crown Publishers, 1984.

Weidensaul, Scott. *Hummingbirds.* New York: Portland House, 1989.

Index